MW01260092

Advance Praise for

SPARK BRILLIANCE FOR EDUCATORS

"Spark Brilliance for Educators is the essential guide for teachers who don't just want to adapt to the future—they want to help shape it."

—DAG KITTLAUS, Co-Founder & CEO of Siri

"Spark Brilliance for Educators brings positive psychology to life in classrooms, giving teachers the tools to cultivate trust, ignite a love of learning, and help students grow into their full potential."

—SHAWN ACHOR, New York Times bestselling author of The Happiness Advantage and Big Potential

"Jackie Insinger and Monica White demonstrate a deep understanding of the principles of positive psychology and their application in the modern classroom. The authors took Jackie's established outstanding leadership playbook for corporate executives and reimagined it to create a nationwide movement to give teachers, every teacher, the ability and proven practical steps to build trustworthy relationships that SPARK students to uncover their own brilliance."

—DR. NANCY S. GRASMICK, Former State Superintendent of Maryland Public Schools

"Brilliance isn't rare—it emerges when the right conditions are in place. Clarity sparks confidence. Connection fuels learning. Small wins build momentum. In Spark Brilliance for Educators, Jackie Insinger and Monica White show how small, intentional shifts can transform the way students see themselves and their potential—creating lasting impact in the classroom and beyond."

—SHAWNA WELLS, 7Gen Legacy Group

"Spark Brilliance for Educators is a research-backed guide for teachers who want to create a learning environment where students feel seen, respected, and understood—exactly what research shows kids need today. With actionable strategies rooted in relationships, motivation, and positive psychology, this book is a must-read for educators looking to make a meaningful difference."

—MEGAN L. SMITH, PH.D, Associate Profession School of Public and Population Health Boise State University

"Relationships are critical in education, and sometimes they are hard to make. Personalities can be so different. Spark Brilliance for Educators provides "aha" moments and doable suggestions that provide educators with a different lens, allowing them to make meaningful shifts in their interactions with students and colleagues immediately."

—LISA BOYD, Superintendent, Idaho School district

"Spark Brilliance for Educators is a research-backed guide for teachers who want to create a learning environment where students feel seen, respected, and understood—exactly what research shows kids need today. With actionable strategies rooted in relationships, motivation, and positive psychology, this book is a must-read for educators looking to make a meaningful difference."

—REBECCA WHEELER, Middle School Teacher

A TEACHER'S PLAYBOOK

SPARK
BRILLIANCE
FOR EDUCATORS

IGNITE, ENGAGE, AND
TRANSFORM YOUR CLASSROOM

JACKIE INSINGER
WITH MONICA WHITE

**SPARK
UNIVERSE
MEDIA**

SPARK BRILLIANCE FOR EDUCATORS

Ignite, Engage, and Transform Your Classroom

ISBN   978-1-962341-66-0   *Hardcover*

        978-1-962341-65-3   *Paperback*

        978-1-962341-67-7   *Ebook*

For the educators who show up every day—exhausted, inspired, determined—because you believe in the brilliance of your students, even when they don't see it yet. This is for you.

CONTENTS

INTRODUCTION

"It begins with us!"

Typically, a five a.m. phone call from a friend is a cause for concern, or at the very least an examination of your phone's Do Not Disturb settings. But that morning, when my dear friend Monica White called me with an idea that had literally woken her from a deep sleep, I could hear something in her voice that made me sit up and listen.

Excitement. Conviction. A *spark*.

It all started eighteen months before that early-morning call, when my amazing sister-in-law, Tina, reached out to me about giving her lifelong friend Monica a sneak peek at the book I was getting ready to publish, *Spark Brilliance*. "She really wants to read your manuscript," Tina told me.

Really? I thought. *Why?*

Monica wasn't exactly the target audience for a book about corporate leadership; as a leading expert in education with years of experience as a teacher, school principal, and now co-founder and CEO of a massively successful charter school system, I had to wonder how a data-driven book about transformative leadership would land with her. But Monica and I had been good friends ever since we bonded years ago at Tina's bachelorette party, so she seemed like a great person to send an advance copy of my manuscript—and I was eager for her feedback (after all, all feedback is good feedback, right?).

When Monica read it, her reaction was beyond anything I expected. She was floored. That was her exact word: "floored." She called me as soon as she was done reading, her voice shaking with excitement.

"Jackie," she said, "this has the potential to change everything."

I laughed nervously. "That's the hope."

"No," she insisted, "you don't understand. This made me rethink so many of my own decisions and interactions over the years. I'm buying this for my entire staff."

The "staff" she was talking about was the dedicated team at Elevate Academy, a network of multiple Career Technical Public Charter Schools serving at-risk students in Idaho. True to her word, the week the book launched, Monica bought copies for every principal, teacher, and administrator at Elevate. It was overwhelming in the best way. I was thrilled that the Spark framework, which I had designed for a corporate audience, seemed to have a broader application. The world of education wasn't something I had a ton of contact with, besides being the mom of two precocious boys in the public school system; it was surprising and incredibly exciting to see Monica so taken with the content. I'd been so focused on the corporate world that it hadn't even occurred to me that other industries might get some benefit out of the concepts in the book.

Monica flew out for my book launch party, a gesture that I found incredibly touching, while also being surprised once again at the depth of her interest in Spark. As I stood in front of the gathered crowd and answered questions about the book, I could see her standing near the back of the room, clutching her copy; I didn't know it at the time, but the ideas you're going to learn in this book were already brewing inside her head. With Spark, Monica didn't just see possibilities; she saw pathways.

"This," she said after the panel, as we sipped our celebratory champagne, "is exactly what we need in education. Not just for our leaders, but for *every* educator."

I had just become a published author, the book was already blowing up my inbox with leadership training opportunities, and I was at the beginning of a wonderfully long and continuing season of spreading the message of *Spark Brilliance* on every stage, podcast, and conference room that I could fit into my calendar. I had, let's just say, a *very* full plate.

And if you had asked me then, I *never* would have been able to imagine everything that's led to the book you now hold in your hands.

THE MISSING PIECE

Spark Brilliance was published in 2022 as a leadership playbook for executives rooted in the principles of Positive Psychology. The Spark framework is built around a core concept: that as a leader, the brilliance, engagement, success, performance, and fulfillment of the people you lead "begins with you".

Spark Brilliance reached a far bigger audience than I could have imagined. When I was in the trenches of writing it, I was hopeful that *anyone* would read it, let alone the tens of thousands of people who have been impacted by it in over twenty countries in the years since. In fact, when my editor asked me one day during the writing process what success would look like to me, I answered: "Someone I don't know telling me they actually read my book!" (I was reassured that this was a given, and that I could safely aim *slightly* higher with my aspirations.)

The overwhelming positive reaction when the book came out was a huge boost and validation of the whole Spark concept. I remember thinking: *Wow. Twenty years developing this was absolutely worth it. Spark REALLY works.*

But, again, my whole world was corporate leadership; I was steeped in executive coaching and leadership team sessions. So when Monica asked me to run the Spark Leadership Accelerator for her entire Elevate leadership team, including the principals and assistant principals at her many schools, I was optimistic (as you'll learn throughout this book, that tends to be my default state)—but also a little trepidatious. Would this really work for educators?

The Accelerator was intense, and Monica's team showed up. They dug deep, leaned into the discomfort, and started seeing results. *Quickly.*

Monica wasn't just satisfied; she was lit up by the results she was seeing. She had co-founded Elevate in 2019 after becoming increasingly frustrated by the outcomes and opportunities for at-risk kids in the traditional public schools where she held leadership positions. The improvements in student success were immediately apparent, and with Spark, she was seeing a way to accelerate those positive outcomes even more. Even just between staff, administrators, and teachers, Spark was a game changer.

And she didn't want to stop there.

"This idea started keeping me up at night," she told me. "In education, we're always taught that building relationships of trust and connection with students has a huge impact on their performance. Everything we want to happen, happens, when students feel seen and significant—higher attendance, faster learning, better test scores, you name it. But we've always struggled with the *how*. How can teachers build those relationships? What are the building blocks? What are the tools? There's a piece missing from teacher training. This isn't something they're taught—and yet they're told it's critical to the outcomes we're aiming for."

Some teachers, she explained to me, just *have* it. They naturally know how to build those relationships—either through innate ability or years of experience.

"But we can't just leave it up to chance that a teacher is going to naturally understand how to do it. We need a system. We need a framework and a methodology that teachers can use, repeatably, reliably, with *every* kid, no matter what's happening in the classroom or in their life."

Unfortunately, this system didn't exist.

…until that 5 a.m. phone call.

"What if we taught teachers to use Spark with students?" Monica asked. I could practically hear the excitement crackling over the phone line.

I sat up in bed, rubbing the sleep out of my eyes. "You mean adapt the Spark Leadership Accelerator for classrooms?"

"Exactly," she said. "It's like you say in the book. It begins with us! Now that all the Elevate teachers know Spark, imagine if they spread that spark to their students. Imagine the impact."

I'd be lying if I said I wasn't skeptical. The Spark Leadership Accelerator had been designed for corporate leaders, who are managing relationships with adult employees. Would it even translate to the classroom with kids?

"Jackie," Monica said, "what if this is the missing piece?"

Far be it from me to respond to a statement like *that* with anything but a *heck yeah!*

"I'm in," I said, feeling a mix of excitement and terror.

We got to work immediately, pulling together a Spark pilot program. Elevate was the perfect testing ground. Monica rallied her team, and we brought in a top independent university researcher to measure the impact, got a control school set up, and went to work. We wanted to know, definitively, if this crazy idea could work.

I'll cut to the chase—*it did.*

When the research results from the Spark pilot program came back, they stopped us in our tracks. The data wasn't just good; it was *transformative.* The outcomes were so significant they felt almost surreal, like we had stumbled onto something much bigger than we'd anticipated. *The missing piece!*

The results from the pilot were undeniable. The same principles that transformed Monica's leadership team were having a profound effect on the students. Engagement levels shot up. Behavioral issues declined. Even the teachers reported feeling more connected and empowered; their burnout went down as student attendance and test scores went up. We quickly realized the potential impact of Spark—and that it needed structure, scalability, and a plan to reach more teachers.

Spark wasn't just a one-time experiment. It was a movement in the making.

On the strength of the first pilot, we secured a sizable grant from an education fund—sizable enough that we could bring in an expert team of instructional designers to help create a program designed specifically for teachers and students. This second pilot program would be run at scale, across all the Elevate Academies. Fueled by the blood, sweat, and tears of the whole Spark team, we launched Version 2 of our pilot in August 2024.

The results are what you hold in your hands. (Spoiler alert: the Version 2 results were *even more mind-blowing*, so buckle up!)

In fact, soon after this book is published, Spark will have completed a third pilot, launched a Spark Educators certification program, and been officially rolled out in a select group of Spark schools across the country. Less than two years after Monica's 5 a.m. phone call, Spark will be brought to thousands of students nationwide.

IT BEGINS WITH YOU

As a teacher, your students' brilliance begins with you. If you can create a learning environment where students feel seen, respected, and understood; where they're guided to identify and nurture their passions; where they form healthy relationships through alignment, communication, and bonding; and where they come to powerfully believe in themselves as beings of limitless potential, you can drive forward their performance and outcomes at a far greater level.

Monica and I wrote this book to serve two purposes.

First: we've seen firsthand the incredible impact Spark has made in classrooms so far, and we want to fan that spark into a flame that begins with each teacher who reads this book.

Second: we want to give you practical steps you can take to bring Spark into your classroom *right now*. You don't need to rewrite your whole curriculum. You can get started today.

One of the most exciting aspects of Spark is that it's designed to work for every teacher in all K-12 schools, from public to private to charter and beyond, regardless of experience. It's a system, a toolkit, and a mindset all in one. For the seasoned educator, it refines and enhances the skills they already have, offering a streamlined way to dig deeper without burning out. For the newer teacher, it provides a blueprint to build meaningful connections and effective practices right from the start.

At its core, the Spark framework is about showing up—not perfectly, but fully. It's about recognizing that your presence, your mindset, and your energy are some of the most powerful tools you have as a teacher.

Sometimes, students can't articulate what they're feeling. They might not even know why they're shutting down or acting out. Every student has layers of complexity we may not see at first glance. And when we take the time to connect with those layers, we don't just help them graduate; we help them thrive. That's the essence of Spark—seeing the unseen, asking the deeper questions, and supporting students as they uncover their own brilliance.

And that's what this book is really about: *brilliance*.

Brilliance in all aspects of our experience as educators: our relationships with students, and our nurturing of their talent, performance, and outlook.

Brilliance that begins with one spark: you.

In this book, you'll learn how to spark brilliance in students by building relationships on the following fundamentals:

1. **The Platinum Rule:** Discovering how to treat students not how *you* want to be treated, but how *they* want to be treated.

2. **Understanding:** Fluid, clear, and mutually understood communication.

3. **Alignment:** Getting on the same page about expectations.

4. **Connection:** Building true authenticity with students.

5. **Brilliance:** Helping students find their spark—what lights them up and brings them alive.

6. **Trust:** Creating and maintaining a classroom environment of

psychological safety.

7. **Growth:** The process of safely getting stretchy to grow into new potential.

8. **Celebrating Wins:** How to motivate students with small victories.

9. **Play:** Bringing the oxytocin-rich bonding experience of *fun* into the classroom!

10. **Gratitude:** It's not just a journaling exercise. With gratitude, you can literally change how you (and your students) see and show up in the world.

Some of these may be familiar to you already. But stay with me: the framework of mindsets and actions you'll learn in this book will feel revolutionary. Most importantly, it will feel *achievable*. You can definitely do this.

Put together in the Spark framework, the ten fundamentals you'll learn in this book create an invisible layer of relationship-building with your students that will not only skyrocket their performance and outcomes, but will also teach them the invaluable lessons of humanity that are so often missing from mandated curricula—how to build meaningful, enriching relationships in the years to come after they leave your classroom.

Through my experience with Monica, the rest of the Spark educators at Elevate, and all of the great teachers I've been blessed to know, I understand that time is a big deal for teachers. Educators often feel like they're drowning in an endless to-do list, juggling lesson plans, grading, administrative tasks, and, of course, the unpredictable needs and behaviors of their students. So, as you're reading this book, it's totally understandable if your first reaction might be: "I don't have time for this!"

Here's the thing: you don't have time *not* to do this. Bringing Spark into your classroom requires an upfront investment of time to learn and implement. But the return on that investment? It's massive.

When you take the time to lay the foundation with Spark, you're not just checking another box on your to-do list. You're building a framework that will fundamentally shift the way you connect with your students. That connection creates a ripple effect: fewer struggles, more engagement, and happier students—plus hard metrics like greatly improved attendance and test scores. Instead of spending months pushing and pulling to get through to your students, you start seeing results faster and with less resistance.

Each student is more than a test score or a seat in a classroom—if you're reading this book, you know this all too well. They are whole people with unique strengths, motivations, and sparks. An educator's job is to find those sparks and amplify them into fireworks. When we teach to the whole student—honoring their intelligences, motivations, and interests— we create classrooms where learning is joyful and meaningful. And in doing so, we not only help students excel academically but also prepare them to navigate the world as confident, self-aware, and engaged individuals.

While Spark is designed with the teacher-student relationship in mind, its principles have the potential to transform all of your professional relationships. Think about the other audiences you engage with daily—fellow teachers, administrators, even parents. These relationships can often feel just as challenging as working with students. By extending Spark to those interactions, you're not just improving your teaching; you're enhancing your entire education ecosystem. If you're a teacher, you'll transform your own teaching and the performance of your students; and if you're an administrator, you'll also drastically improve results for your entire school.

Monica and I have believed from the beginning with all our hearts that Spark truly is *the* missing piece that will revolutionize education. Now, thanks to the data from our pilot programs, movers and shakers within the education realm—education funds, national associations, and highly influential educators and influencers—hold the same belief. Their overwhelmingly positive reactions to Spark cemented our confidence. As Monica put it, "So we're not crazy after all—Spark really *is* the missing piece!"

You can spark connection, creativity, and joy in your classroom. The framework you'll learn in this book will show you how to develop the deep, trusting relationships with students that will transform their outcomes and their entire lives.

And as the teacher, it begins with you.

1

DISCOVER

"Ms. Larson, am I going to fail?"

Sophia, one of the brightest students in her tenth-grade geometry class, stood at Beth Larson's desk with tears in her eyes. She'd crept up the rows of desks after class like she was dreading the conversation, and yet now, in front of her teacher, the question had quickly tumbled out in an anxious rush. It was the *last* thing Beth had expected Sophia to say.

"When she asked if she could talk to me after class, I assumed it had to do with her home situation," Beth told a Zoom call filled with the faces of her fellow Spark teachers on one of our weekly roundtable discussions. She was recounting the story to us a couple of weeks after her interaction with Sophia. "We'd been informed that there were custody issues happening between her parents. I was a child of divorce—I know what that's like. I had been watching her all semester to see signs of stress, but so far, she was managing it like it wasn't happening."

If anything, Sophia had been doing *better* at her schoolwork since the trouble at home had started. This was high praise, too, since Sophia was an excellent student. "Let's put it this way: when I'm grading her stuff, I don't even bother uncapping my red pen," Beth told us.

"Why on earth would you think you're going to fail?" Beth asked Sophia. "You're doing great!"

Sophia looked unconvinced. "Well," she said hesitantly, "you didn't give me an extra credit assignment like you gave everyone else. And I saw Charlie's take-home quiz from last week. He had a whole other page of questions I didn't have. And you let me have extra time on the test even when you told everyone there was no extra time…"

Of course I did, kid—you have enough on your plate. Sophia wasn't being paranoid; Beth had definitely been quietly reducing her student's workload over the past several weeks. *Just like Mr. Mellin did for me.*

"Child of divorce" didn't really evoke the full extent of what Beth had endured during her junior year of high school. The stress at home had only amplified the stress at school, a particularly stressful year of tough courses meant to boost her college applications. Sleep, regular meals, and socializing had been in short order as she put everything she had into trying to get a 4.0 GPA so she could escape her home life to college as soon as possible.

And then her calculus teacher, Mr. Mellin—not even her favorite teacher, nor one she was particularly close to—had started gently reducing her workload. It was subtle, but Beth was so attuned to the workload that she noticed right away; a waived quiz here, an extension there. She knew he wasn't doing it for the other kids in the class.

It made a world of difference to Beth. It meant catching up on sleep; breathing room to hang out with friends on occasion. The reduction in stress had a huge impact on her overall mental state the rest of her junior year, allowing her to get through with the GPA that would land her an acceptance and scholarship at her dream school.

Now, knowing what Sophia was going through, Beth was only too happy to pass on the kindness and care Mr. Mellin had shown her. Sophia hadn't asked for a single bit of help, but Beth knew it would make a big difference, so she gave it.

"And it did make a big difference," Beth told us on the roundtable call. "Just not in the direction I intended."

Sophia listed out all the small ways Beth had reduced her workload, and gulped nervously before saying in a near-whisper, "Are you just giving up on me?"

"Sophia, why would you think that? I would never give up on you, or any student. And you've gotten straight As on every single test and assignment all year."

"You used to give me really hard stuff. You gave me extra work. Now you give me the same work that the kids in the non-gifted classes get. Is it because I stopped doing good on the work? Are you making it easier for me because I'm doing bad? Am I not in the gifted class anymore? *Am I going to fail?"*

Oh.

Beth found herself flashing back to the summer of 2015, when her two kids had convinced her to do the Ice Bucket Challenge—the same ice-cold jolt of instant regret was washing through her.

Sophia didn't see the lightening of her coursework as a welcome reduction in stress. If anything, it had *added* to her stress because she thought it meant she was hopelessly out of her element and her teacher was taking pity on her.

"Yeah, so, that Platinum Rule we always talk about in Spark?" Beth told us on the roundtable call, a rueful grin on her face. "Turns out *it's a little important!*"

WHAT IS POSITIVE PSYCHOLOGY?

Before we dive further into this chapter, let's cover some background context that will inform everything you read in this book. In fact, it's the backbone of the Spark program: *Positive Psychology.*

Positive Psychology is the scientific study of what makes life most worth living. This is a short definition of a field that is more defined by its broadness and potential than by any attempt to contain it within a few succinct words. What I love about this definition is that it is itself open and far-reaching, making space for a multitude of interpretations, endless avenues of impact.

When asked by friends, colleagues, and clients, I define Positive Psychology as the science of *potential.* And here's how we'll use it together in this book.

Picture a line of numbers with zero in the middle, negative numbers to the left, and positive numbers to the right. When we typically think of our "baseline" as individuals—our sea level of happiness, performance, engagement, and perspective—we place it at zero on the line. When we're feeling low in these areas, we dip below the baseline into the negative numbers.

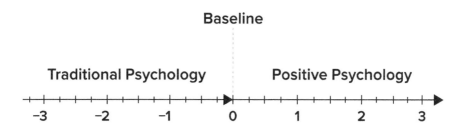

Traditional psychology is the study of those dips, and the practice of healing by bringing people out of the negative numbers back up to their baseline. That's the goal: equilibrium, sea level.

But there's an infinite stretch of positive numbers extending past baseline. How does one keep moving forward?

Positive Psychology is the study and practice of the positive numbers. To me, it's not an *alternative* or *contrast* to traditional psychology; rather, it's a continuation of its impact, the "what's next" sought by a person who has achieved equilibrium. The absence of negative doesn't equal positive; the absence of sickness doesn't equal health. When it comes to your mindset, the absence of sadness doesn't equal happiness. When it comes to your team, the absence of poor performance doesn't equal great performance. Neutral is merely the starting point where great things become possible—not the final destination.

And yet so often, we're stuck in neutral. I see this day after day, not only in my work but with people in my life as well—everyone from friends to family to strangers in the grocery store. I see behaviors and attitudes that suggest a belief that neutral is all we can hope for. Surviving, not thriving.

Happy is quite a reach; let's just get to *not sad* and call it good, okay?

The father of Positive Psychology, Martin Seligman, carved out the field in the late 1990s as a rebuttal to that idea. Seligman and psychologist Christopher Peterson's *Character Strengths and Virtues: A Handbook and Classification*, became the seminal text in a new field of scientific inquiry: what goes *right*, rather than *wrong*, with people's psychology.

It strikes me as amazing that we went so long as curious beings focused on studying the negative in the field of psychology, rather than the positive. But then, as humans, we're hardwired to focus on survival, which involves doggedly seeking out the *bad* in order to fix or avoid it. Biologically, our cognitive bias is to see the negative—because, sure, that shadow over in the corner of our cave *might* be nothing, but it also might be a bear. We wouldn't have survived as a species if we *didn't* treat every shadow like a bear.

But in our modern world, seeing the bear in every shadow actually holds us back. We now have the privilege and the opportunity to choose *not* to see the bear.

I see the stretch of numbers to the right of zero as a road of endless potential. In those positive numbers is joy; creativity; fulfillment; excitement. It's where we experience the deepest connections with each other and where we show up best for everyone in our lives. It's where our performance multiplies and shines outward, not just as individuals, but as teams.

And in the education world, where attention is often focused on "what's wrong" that needs to be "fixed", it's easy for teachers to get parked in the numbers to the *left* of zero. But the numbers to the right of zero represent limitless opportunity for your students.

What we've seen with Spark teachers is that, by shifting their attention—and their students' attention—into the positive numbers, the entire mood of the learning space opens up. The students see themselves not as victims of past circumstance, but active, empowered participants in their own future. *They get to choose* how they see the world and how they show up.

THE PLATINUM RULE

Above all, Positive Psychology is about perspective.

Its greatest benefit, and its greatest potential, lie in its foundational premise that we have power over our perspective, that it's something we can observe, consider, and change. We can choose how we see and experience the world. We can choose how we show up in each moment.

This is incredibly important for how we interact with other people. If each of us has a perspective that is fluid rather than fixed, this means there is no one "right" perspective. Each person's perspective is unique and equally valid.

You're probably thinking: *this isn't news*.

And you're right. It's one of those things we hear constantly—*everyone has their own perspective*. Sure. That's a given.

Then why don't we live that way?

So much of our behavior and interactions as a society speak to the opposite belief, that perception is fixed, and that reality *is* our perception. We perceive something, and *that's how it happened*. We focus inward on our personal experience of each moment and guard our perspective like it's the key piece of evidence in the trial of the century.

This self-focus imbues not only our actions but also our guidelines for interaction. For example, take one of the most well-known "rules" for how to interact with other people: the Golden Rule.

Treat others the way you want to be treated.

Key word: *you*. The way *you* want to be treated.

Who says the way you want to be treated is the way everyone else wants to be treated?

You know that one well-meaning family member who's just a little out of touch, and when the holidays roll around, they hand out gifts that are what they themselves would *love* to receive, but that leave the recipients befuddled? A ten-year-old unwrapping a gift card for a facial instead of the Xbox game they were hoping for —that's what comes to mind when I think of the Golden Rule.

The Golden Rule is premised on the assumption that your personal perspective is the same as everyone else's. That your deepest wants and needs are exactly the same as the deepest wants and needs of everyone you interact with.

Putting it that way, it's obvious why it doesn't work very well, isn't it?

The Golden Rule keeps us focused on our own wants and needs, when as leaders, our success lies in the wants and needs of the people we serve. Yet the Golden Rule is still at the top of the list when we talk about best practices in relationships. We *know* our own perspective isn't the same as everyone else's, but we follow a practice that keeps us focused on ourselves, rather than the people we're trying to connect with.

Early on in grad school, before I would start to develop the model I would later introduce to thousands of people, I came across a different rule: the Platinum Rule.

It was so simple, and at the same time, it blew my mind.

Treat other people the way they want to be treated.

I thought, *Oh wow, that's genius!*

Then in the next split second, I thought: *Well, duh. Of course.*

It was a strange, dissonant moment. My brain seemed to be having a breakthrough on a new concept, and yet when I really thought about it, it was so obvious that I assumed I must already know it.

You may experience the same feeling as you read through this book, because the Platinum Rule is the starting point for each part of the Spark framework. It's the thread that brings it all together, and it works because it reaches in and grabs hold of one of our deepest desires as humans:

We want to be *known*.

CRACKING THE CODE

As an educator, your job is to support, nourish, and empower the potential and performance of the students you teach.

In my experience working with educators in the Spark program, I've seen firsthand that teachers take that responsibility ultraseriously. Besides coffee, it's often the first thing they think about when they roll out of bed in the morning: *how can I bring out the absolute best in my students?*

But they also report that sometimes it feels like the Sunday crossword, a puzzle they stare at for hours on end, unable to crack: *how can I possibly know what will motivate each student best, and where on Earth would I find the time to discover that?*

Research consistently shows that high school students perform better academically when they feel seen, supported, and have a strong sense of belonging within their school community. Students who feel a sense of belonging are more motivated to learn, achieve higher academic success, and have a positive future orientation. The opposite is *also* true: students who feel like they don't belong, who feel unseen or misunderstood, show negative impacts on academic performance and overall well-being.[1]

This is especially important for educators to be aware of right now— because unfortunately, students' sense of "belonging" is at an all-time low. A Qualtrics survey from 2022 showed that only 51% of students feel like they belong at school. They cite a disconnection from peers and teachers, largely due to aftereffects from the pandemic, as a major reason why.

So that means fully *half* of students are feeling disconnected and unsupported. I'd bet this comes as no surprise to most educators. However,

---

[1] https://ies.ed.gov/ncee/rel/Products/Region/northwest/Ask-A-REL/60072

often when teachers are faced with a student who needs support, their instinctive reaction is to craft that support through the lens of what makes *them* feel supported. As humans, our instinct is the Golden Rule—treating others how *we* want to be treated—when we're better served by the Platinum Rule—treat others how *they* want to be treated.

Have you ever seen the *Friends* episode where Ross decides to wear some "edgy" leather pants on a date? Everything's going great until he starts to overheat, goes to his date's bathroom to take the pants off and cool down, and, well…things start going wrong. He can't get the pants back on. He tries baby powder—no dice. He squirts lotion all over the baby powder—pants are still stuck. By the end of the scene, he's forced to exit the bathroom pantsless, covered in a powder-lotion paste, holding the leather pants sheepishly, to the horror of his date (who, predictably, does *not* want to see him again).

Using the Golden Rule to support others can feel like that sometimes—every move we make to fix the problem just makes a bigger mess.

That's exactly what Beth had accidentally done with Sophia. She saw a student that reminded her of herself at that age—and brought to mind what she had seen as a welcome relief from her teacher Mr. Mellin, a moment of him seeing, understanding, and caring for her. But Sophia didn't see it that way. In fact, she couldn't have seen it more differently. To Sophia, school was the one place that was *normal*. It was the one place where she felt in control. It was where she went to escape the problems she was having at home; a place where she felt safe, confident, and like she had the respect of her teachers. Her work had been her saving grace.

And then Beth had come in with the Golden Rule and turned that safe space into a world of insecurity, anxiety, and the crushing realization that she was *obviously* failing at the *one* thing that was keeping her grounded.

I'll bet you've been right where Beth was at some point in your education career: trying to help a student with all the best intentions, only to have those very efforts cause an even bigger disconnect. After all, as an educator, your instinct when you see a problem with a student is to help.

But the way *you* see help isn't the way everyone else sees it. It's not always so clear-cut how our communication is received. If what's heard by a student is different from your intentions, you don't always know it right away. A low simmer of discontent can remain unseen for months.

In order to truly help someone, you first have to discover how *they* see help. Only then can you craft the support they will be able to gratefully receive—the kind of support that will make them feel personally cared for.

This is the crux of the Platinum Rule: treat others how *they* want to be treated, not how *you* want to be treated.

UNDERSTAND SOMEBODY ELSE'S UNDERSTANDING

Let's rewind briefly to the moment in grad school when I discovered the Platinum Rule.

I had come across the Platinum Rule early on in some of the pre-course reading I'd been doing. The specific wording came from the work of acclaimed communication researcher Milton Bennett. The deep reinforcement of the concept, however, came from the experience I had in my favorite class during my first semester in the program. It was a profoundly transformative moment, and its impact has been foundational to my career and relationships.

I remember this moment so clearly not just because of how much my mind was blown, but also because of the class itself, and the phenomenal professor who was teaching it: Dr. Eleanor Duckworth, a famous psychologist who studied under Piaget and was instrumental in groundbreaking pedagogy and curriculum development work in the 1960s.

Since I was in a self-designed master's program, I had been able to line up classes with all my academic heroes. In doing so, I was expected to contribute something original to their research during my time in their courses. It was nerve-racking, but thrilling. And the class I was by far the most eagerly anticipating was Dr. Duckworth's. As far as the world of psychology goes, Dr. Duckworth is a superstar. It was like taking a basketball lesson with Michael Jordan. I was totally starstruck.

The first day of class, butterflies in my stomach, I walked into the lecture hall and was immediately handed a journal by Dr. Duckworth's TA. I went to a seat in the front row and settled in as Dr. Duckworth began to take us through the syllabus.

Eventually, she got around to mentioning the journal we'd been handed. "In addition to your coursework," she began, and I swallowed—*in addition?* This was Harvard. The load wasn't exactly light. "…each night, I want you to look at the moon and capture what you see in this journal. You can draw a picture of it, write a poem about it—however you see it. The only requirement is that every single night, you capture something *new* about it."

I felt frustration settle across my shoulders like a wet blanket. *Draw?*

Poetry? I was (and still am) incredibly artistically challenged. I didn't understand why she wanted us to draw the moon. And I knew my output would be...let's just say, *not* my best work.

The assignment was intimidating, and I was annoyed. But, clinging to my innate optimism, I told myself that there were exactly 105 nights coming up in the semester, and so I was going to nail the assignment in quantity at the very least.

Over the course of that fall and early winter, you could always tell a Duckworth student by the way we could be found wandering the campus at night staring up at the polluted Boston sky, trying to find the moon, then trying to write or draw anything about it in our identical journals. By the end of the semester, I had managed to capture all 105 nights of moons. My renderings ranged from vaguely interesting (one night I drew the reflection of the moon in a sidewalk puddle, the most artistic I have ever been and likely ever will be) to "what the heck *is that*" (any attempt at realism, and one misguided stab at a sonnet).

We turned in our journals the Friday before the last week of classes, and the following week, when we entered the lecture hall for our last class with Dr. Duckworth, the entire space was wallpapered edge to edge, floor to ceiling, with our moon captures. Thousands of journal pages, every surface completely covered.

Dr. Duckworth said to us, "Of everything you've learned in my class this term, what I want you to take away most is this. In just three months, we all captured *thousands* of ways to see the same object—the moon."

We all looked around in awe. The same flash of insight was clearly occurring to all of us: what we were seeing was the vast universe of human perspectives, all centered on the same unchanging object.

"Prior to this class, you might have assumed the moon could only be seen in one obvious way, and that everyone obviously sees it that way. But look around you. There are thousands of ways to see the moon, each one unique. Each one represents one person's understanding of the moon on one particular night. No two are the same."

Even just in the patch of wall right in front of where I stood, there were wildly divergent versions of the moon. The sheer difference from page to page was astounding.

"What I'm trying to teach you, and what I want you to take away from this class," Dr. Duckworth concluded, "is the idea of *understanding somebody else's understanding.*"

It was a famous saying of hers, one that I recognized from her writing. In that moment, everything clicked for me, like a flash of light—like a spark.

It had never occurred to me that there was more than one way to see the moon. That everyone didn't see it as I saw it.

But my classmates and I had managed to find a kaleidoscope of views of that same single object. We had come up with thousands of lenses to look through.

That day was when the Platinum Rule lodged itself in my head and set me on the course of what would become my career. The value of understanding somebody else's understanding was tremendous and crucial if I hope to understand people, and in doing so, leverage that understanding into more meaningful relationships.

Treat others as they want to be treated. I could only do that if I shattered my assumptions—which were based on my own perspective—and focused on discovering each individual's unique lens. Each new view of the moon was an opportunity for a new connection.

THE FALSE CONSENSUS EFFECT

So, why *do* our minds so commonly default to our own perceptions and preferences?

Well, that's easy: the way we perceive the world is the only reference point we have. As a result, our preferences and behavior are what we naturally assume others will share.

This phenomenon has a name: *the false-consensus effect*. When people are asked to guess how others will behave in a given situation, by and large, they vastly overestimate how many other people will share their beliefs, preferences, judgments, and reactions. More than that, they're often surprised when their perspective isn't shared. They assume that a different viewpoint must be rare.

It's like how people say, "*Everyone* knows that!" when something they believe is a fact is challenged. They're often surprised that, no, *not* everyone knows or even agrees, and the percentage who do know or agree is much, much lower than they assume.

Social psychologist Brett Pelham writes:

The need to belong (the desire to be accepted and connected to others) nudges people toward false-consensus effects. That is, we overestimate consensus for our own attitudes and behavior because we assume that other people who share our opinions are more likely to accept us. In a sense, then, the false consensus effect is a form of wishful social thinking. It's reassuring to think that people agree with us.[2]

With all this in mind, it's no wonder that when trying to create moments of connection in the classroom—when reaching out a hand to students in service and support—teachers often rely on the only reference point we have: how *they* feel served and supported.

As an educator, your most powerful tool is the Platinum Rule. Teachers who put it to use in the Spark program reported massive shifts in classroom culture as a result:

- "I find myself using it on the daily. It's completely turned around the classroom environment."

- "It's so helpful to have language to use to describe how we should all be treating each other. I've seen the kids really take on Platinum with each other, peer to peer, as a result."

- "They actually liked being asked about themselves once I premised it with wanting to help them be more comfortable in the classroom. They opened up about things I would never have had any idea about."

This one mindset shift is such a game changer, and so foundational to

---

2 Brett Pelham, "Your Opinions Are Not as Popular as You Think They Are: The False Consensus Effect," Character and Context (blog), Society for Personality and Social Psychology, October 25, 2019, https://www.spsp.org/news-center/blog/pelham-false-con-sensus.

all the other methods we'll cover in this book, that it should be the first question you ask in any classroom situation.

How do they want to be treated?

If you don't know the answer, your job as an educator is to find out.

Key Concept: Emotional Contagion

We know that the entire classroom will pick up on each other's negativity, anxiety, and stress, and with no one is this more true than with their leader—you, the teacher.

The best way to make the concept of emotional contagion click for someone is to tell them, "Imagine yawning."

There—you just yawned, didn't you?

Much to the delight of kids throughout the ages, the act of yawning is probably the most universally recognized as wickedly contagious for seemingly no good reason. You look at someone yawning, you yawn. You think of someone yawning, you yawn. You can't help it. And if you try not to yawn, the impulse just gets worse.

It turns out that emotions function in almost exactly the same way and are just as contagious. Emotional contagion is the spontaneous transfer of emotions from one person to another or through a group. It was first written about back in 1911 by American psychologist James Baldwin, who called the phenomenon "contagion of feeling."[3]

Throughout the past century, it was studied in countless ways, and in 1993, psychologists Elaine Hatfield, John Cacioppo, and Richard Rapson pinned down the concept as "the tendency to automatically mimic and synchronize expressions, vocalizations, postures, and movements with those of another person's and consequently, to converge emotionally."[4]

Researchers have documented how, as we pass through the day, our brains continually process the feelings of those around us. We notice the inflection of their voice, the arch of their eyebrows, the slope of their shoulders. Our amygdala can read and identify emotions in another person's face in 33 milliseconds[5] and almost instantaneously prime us to adopt that emotion as well. This all happens subconsciously, but consciously we're doing the same thing: reading people and feeling the same thing they're feeling. If you put three strangers in a room, the most emotionally expressive individual will transmit their mood to the others within two minutes.

---

3   James Baldwin, The Individual and Society or Psychology and Sociology (Boston: Richard G. Badger, 1911), 44.

4   Elaine Hatfield, John T. Cacioppo, and Richard L. Rapson, "Emotional Contagion," Current Directions in Psychological Science 2 no. 3 (June 1993): 96–99, https://www.jstor.org/stable/20182211.

5   Rachel Feltman, "Your Brain Helps You Judge a Face Before You Even See It," The Washington Post, August 5, 2014, https://www.washingtonpost.com/news/speaking-of-science/wp/2014/08/05/your-brain-helps-you-judge-a-face-before-you-even-see-it/.

So, to put it simply, when someone in a bad mood enters your sphere, you suddenly find yourself in a bad mood, too. The effect is amplified in groups, and it doesn't even require physical presence to occur. In January of 2012, Facebook conducted an experiment (the ethicality of which has been widely debated) that manipulated the content of 689,003 users' news feeds.6 Some people were bombarded with positive news stories, happy life updates, and words that had been determined to be more positive. Other people were shown an onslaught of content that had been categorized as more negative and pessimistic. After a week of this content delivery, the groups of users were prompted to make their own posts. Predictably, those users in the Positive group spontaneously posted more positive status messages; those in the Negative group posted gloom.

If people in digital groups can so easily be infected by emotions, what does that suggest for groups of people who share space every day in a classroom?

With every moment of your interactions with students, you have the opportunity to create a ripple effect with your outlook and emotional state. You have the power to use emotional contagion to the benefit of everyone around you.

---

6 Robinson Meyer, "Everything We Know about Facebook's Secret Mood-Manipulation Experiment," The Atlantic, September 8, 2014, https://www.theatlantic.com/technology/archive/2014/06/everything-we-know-about-facebooks-secret-mood-manipulation-experiment/373648/.

MINING FOR PLATINUM

Discovering how your students want to be treated isn't as cut and dried as simply *asking* someone how they want to be treated (although that's not a bad place to start, and it's certainly where Beth started the next time she saw Sophia).

In the classroom, getting kids to speak up for themselves can feel like pulling teeth. Many students worry that asking for help will lead peers or teachers to see them as incompetent; the fear of being seen as "less than" keeps them from asking for help.[7] This is even more apparent with students from low-income or working-class families who may have been taught not to "bother" teachers, viewing help-seeking as inappropriate.[8]

STUDENTS SPEAK

"Before Spark, I wasn't really paying attention in class or maybe just slacking on my work. But once we started doing the program, I felt like I could actually be myself and start opening up to the teachers."

---

7 https://www.edweek.org/teaching-learning/opinion-the-real-reason-why-students-dont-ask-teachers-for-help/2021/10

8 https://www.aft.org/ae/winter2014-2015/sparks

As a result, using the Platinum Rule can sometimes feel like mining for platinum itself—an intensive process that involves digging in the deep darkness thousands of feet underground and using explosives to blow apart the rigid, packed-in ore.

SPARK STUDY RESULTS

In Spark's first independent study, huge changes were seen in the school's culture and learning environment after the pilot program was implemented—and the impact was obvious in student attendance and teacher retention.

- Student attendance was 12.59% higher with Spark; attendance at the Spark school reached 95.31%—more than five points higher than the national average in 2023 of 90%!

- Another amazing result: Teacher retention at the Spark School was 10% higher than at the Control School.

It can be even more difficult to create this environment with students who are new to your teaching style and learning how to connect with you. They need time to build trust in you, and until they feel that trust, they're often cautious and reserved in volunteering their own needs. You've probably noticed this effect in adults, too—I hear people say all the time that they don't want to "come off as high-maintenance." They even take pride in their ability to "adapt to any situation."

That's usually just another way of saying that they're accustomed to their needs being *assumed*, not *known*.

And therein lies your greatest opportunity. You can show students a new kind of classroom environment, one based on their needs, in a way that forms deeper connections and greater empowerment than they've ever imagined was possible at school.

IT BEGINS WITH YOU

In order to discover how your students want to be treated, you'll begin by asking questions.

But not just any questions. This part takes some thought.

Remember that this is a little like platinum mining—the shiny stuff is buried deep. Simply asking, "What makes you feel fulfilled and valued?" is as likely to return actionable insight as blasting dynamite on the surface of the mine. You're not going to get in deep.

Instead, play detective. Craft questions that break apart the concept of "fulfilled" and "valued" and are easily understood, and just as easily answered. Questions like:

What do you enjoy most about our class?

How do you like to get help on your schoolwork? Is it better to talk one on one, or talk with the whole class?

Who was your favorite teacher you've ever had, and what did they do to make you feel understood?

A student whose wants and needs you're trying to discover might answer some of these questions like this:

I like that you show us a lot of visuals and illustrations so I can understand the topic better.

It's better for me if we talk one on one. I don't understand as well when it's with the whole class.

When my teacher checked in with me on progress as I went, it let me know they understood that I might not always ask for help when I need it.

If you read between the lines, these answers tell you clear as day what makes this student happy, and how they feel most fulfilled. This is a student who doesn't always understand the instructions given to the whole class, but maybe feels shy and embarrassed about asking for help. And they're a verbal processor who needs help sorting out their thoughts to really get to a place of understanding.

With this information, you can tailor interactions you have with them to how *they want to be treated.*

When you lead with the Platinum Rule in the classroom, you'll connect with students by understanding their understanding. They'll feel seen, validated, and deeply fulfilled; their confidence and performance will skyrocket. Most importantly, their trust in you as their teacher will be strengthened exponentially. They'll be more likely to open up to you about what they need in the future—which means you, as their teacher, will be able to do your job that much better.

This isn't where your job ends, though.

Remember, as the teacher, the mindsets and behaviors you want to see in your classroom begin with you.

Do *you* know how you want to be treated?

If you're reading this and you immediately said *of course!* in your mind, stop. Take a moment to reflect on the question.

Do you *really* know how you want to be treated?

Educators are so often focused on the students they serve that any focus on themselves often falls by the wayside.

The Platinum Rule begins with you. The same questions that you craft to mine the platinum deep within each student in your classroom are the same questions you'll begin by asking yourself.

CLASSROOM ACTION PLAN: MINING FOR PLATINUM

After teaching an activity, conduct a class survey to gather student feedback. Ask them what they enjoyed about the lesson and what they didn't?

Create a bell ringer for your class that asks: What makes class go by fast? What makes class go by slow?

Make this an ongoing practice, not just a one-time effort! If you are regularly asking your students for feedback, you are always mining for platinum and discovering what is working for your learners.

Scan here for a downloadable action plan you can take into the classroom!

2

UNDERSTAND

Jordan sat at his desk, head resting in his hands. Around the room, his fellow classmates were furiously scribbling on the quizzes that had been passed out—but Jordan, like so many other times that semester, sat staring at the sheet of paper, his pencil still.

"Jordan, are you doing okay?" Mr. Ellis asked. Jordan nodded quickly, avoiding eye contact.

It was the latest in Jordan's noticeable struggles Mr. Ellis had noticed throughout the semester, which seemed to get worse as the weeks went on. A seventh grader, Jordan had transferred into the school mid-semester, and had initially done fine—and then something had changed, something Mr. Ellis couldn't quite identify. What began as small errors had snowballed into incomplete assignments and missed deadlines. When Mr. Ellis asked how he could help, Jordan looked away, shrugged, and kept his mouth shut. No amount of encouraging notes left on the assignments he turned in seemed to get him to open up. *Let's talk about this. Come see me if you're having trouble.* But Jordan never did.

The breaking point came near the end of the semester with a major book project. Mr. Ellis had spent an entire class period explaining the assignment, breaking it into manageable steps. He handed out a detailed rubric and encouraged everyone to ask questions. When it came time to turn in the project a week later, Jordan had handed in something that looked like it had been copy-pasted right out of Wikipedia—a bland, matter-of-fact plot summary rather than the more in-depth analysis of the book they'd been assigned to read. Mr. Ellis had no choice but to grade it a D and make his expectations for Jordan crystal clear in his note: *Come see me after class.*

After the final bell, Jordan lingered at his desk, watching his classmates file out. Mr. Ellis approached, pulling up a chair. "Jordan, can we talk about your project?" he asked, keeping his tone light.

Jordan nodded, staring at the floor. "I tried," he said quietly. "I guess I didn't really get what you wanted us to do."

Mr. Ellis frowned slightly. "We spent a whole class going over the instructions. If you didn't understand, why didn't you ask questions?"

Shrug.

"What part was confusing, specifically?"

Jordan hesitated, then said, "It *wasn't* confusing. I thought I got it. But I guess I didn't."

Well, that's clear as mud, Mr. Ellis thought, hoping his frustration wasn't showing on his face. He decided to walk through the instructions one by one with Jordan. And when he hit the instruction about analyzing the themes of the assigned reading, he noticed Jordan's brow furrow. "Did you understand this part, about the analysis?"

"Yeah, that's what I did," Jordan insisted.

Jordan had, indeed, *not* done that. The project he'd turned in was a simple, if detailed, summary of each chapter. It was the kind of thing that would have earned him a good grade in elementary school, but Jordan was a seventh grader with a strong GPA and high test scores from his previous school.

"Tell me about how you did the analysis," Mr. Ellis said.

Another shrug. "I did what you said. I read it, and I wrote down what happened."

Weeks later, on a Spark roundtable, Mr. Ellis—or Sam, as we call him—related this moment as the lightbulb going off in his head, and the beginning of his turning point with Jordan.

"I had asked the class to do analysis. Jordan heard me tell the class to do analysis. There was no miscommunication there," he said. "I forgot one important thing, though—does the word *analysis* mean the same thing to both of us?"

Sam had hit a common stumbling block that I see not only with the Spark educators, but nearly every leader and executive I've worked with in my decades-long coaching career.

Hearing someone is not the same as *understanding* them. And as the teacher, it's your job to make sure students don't just hear you, but truly understand you.

ALL AROUND US, ALL THE TIME

The late, great American writer David Foster Wallace opened his now-famous 2005 commencement speech to the graduating class at Kenyon College with the following anecdote:

> There are these two young fish swimming along and they happen to meet an older fish swimming the other way, who nods at them and says "Morning, boys. How's the water?" And the two young fish swim on for a bit, and then eventually one of them looks over at the other and goes "What the hell is water?"[9]

This is how I often think about the concept of interpersonal communication. It's something we all do so constantly, so naturally, that we really don't think about *how* we're doing it.

Have you ever driven to work or the grocery store and realized you had no memory of how you got there? All the turns you took, lanes you crossed, decisions you made to stop or go or merge or check your blind spot… they were so automatic, they disappeared. Yet because of them, and *only* because of them, you arrived.

For teachers, communication is like this—as easy to overlook as it is vital. Because if you don't do it right, you and your students end up at the wrong destination or, sometimes worse, going around in circles. Remember the Griswolds in *European Vacation* stuck driving in the roundabout, and all Clark Griswold can do is point out, "Look, kids…Big Ben… Parliament!" over and over as they make circles till nightfall? Total frus-

---

9 David Foster Wallace, "This Is Water" (speech). 2005 Commencement Address, Kenyon College, Gambier, Ohio, http://bulletin-archive.kenyon.edu/x4280.html.

tration. No one wants that.

Guess where we start? Connection is impossible without fluid, clear, and mutually understood communication. It's often the most immediate, and highest, wall between teachers and the students they work with (and don't worry—we dive into connection in an upcoming chapter).

I just had a really tough conversation, and I don't think it went well.

I just gave a student some feedback, and they reacted terribly. They got so defensive; they shut down.

I have a student who refuses to follow instructions. No matter how clear I am, it's like she's on another planet. I can't figure out what I'm saying wrong.

Does this sound familiar? The common thread in these concerns is uncertainty. The teacher has a gut feeling that the communication was off. But they're not sure why.

They'll say, "I just don't know if they truly understood what I meant."

Our response is simple: "Did you ask?"

It's a forehead-smack moment, and yet it's so often overlooked—if you want to know how someone is hearing or receiving you, the best way to know for sure is to *ask*. In fact, I recommend whenever you're working with someone new to start with questions specifically about communication. You could ask:

- How do you like to hear feedback? (Written or verbally? In the moment, or later on?)

- Can you think of a conversation you had with another teacher that didn't go well for you? What made it not feel good?

- Can you share a time when a tough conversation *did* go well, and what part of it felt good to you?

- Who's your favorite person to talk to, and what makes you enjoy talking to them so much?

These questions establish the baseline of how you want to interact with one another. What a great way to begin to build communication *and* connection.

In classrooms with great communication culture, students and teachers are on the same page. Lessons are clear, expectations are even clearer, and everyone is sure what they're supposed to do next. This clarity builds trust, builds psychological safety, and leads to vastly improved student outcomes.

- A 2017 study conducted in Ireland with 274 teachers found that simply acknowledging students' feelings significantly strength-ened educator-learner relationships and created an autono-my-supportive classroom climate.[10]

- The Harvard Graduate School of Education conducted a randomized field experiment demonstrating that regular commu-nication between teachers and families leads to increased

---

10   (Cheon et al., 2019; Roache & Lewis, 2011; Wallace et al., 2014; Weger, 2017).

student engagement, suggesting that involving families in the communication loop can positively impact students' academic experiences.[11]

Think of it this way: kids spend six to eight hours a day in the classroom, and as any educator or parent knows all too well, they're like behavior sponges. Modeling the kind of great communication skills that will serve them in adulthood is critical for their social and emotional learning. As their teacher, it begins with you. If you can show them that you're constantly seeking to understand them, they'll be more likely to model that behavior back at you, bridging the gap between *hearing* and *understanding*.

STUDENTS SPEAK

"I think it really opened my eyes a lot more to how I'm similar to a lot of people. It helped me see how they're feeling or what they're going through. Spark just opened my eyes."

GROUND RULES FOR GREAT COMMUNICATION

Great teaching begins with great communication. Great communication requires attention, intention, and practice.

---

11 Kraft, M. A., & Dougherty, S. M. (2013). The effect of teacher–family communication on student engagement: Evidence from a randomized field experiment. Journal of Research on Educational Effectiveness, 6(3), 199-222.

Action #1: Assume the Best of Intentions

You're going to be well served entering into *any* interaction by assuming positive intent. Conversely, assuming ill intent can harm your teaching in the long run by eroding the trust you've built with your students.

On our Spark roundtables, we held space for great stories about students—and as expected, the occasional venting. One thing that impressed me about the teachers was their *constant* assumption of good intentions, even when they were frustrated with a student.

"It's like she refuses to listen... but I know she's trying."

"Sometimes it feels like the whole class *wants* to misunderstand me, because then it's not their fault when they do a bad job. But then I remind myself: they want to succeed, and they need me to believe *they want to succeed* in order to get through to them."

Listening to them talk about their students often gave me flashbacks to my own adolescence. I wasn't always sure my teachers cared about me as a person rather than just another head in their classroom; I often felt like they assumed the worst about us as kids, or didn't put much energy into assuming anything at all. Anytime I felt that energy from a teacher, it made me totally disengage. More than that, it made me completely disinterested in the subject they taught. I was a hyper-achiever as a kid, so I still did well in those classes because I cared about my grades—but I didn't connect with the subjects and tended to write them off (like biology; to this day I'm *still* bored by biology). A teacher *not* taking the time to try to understand me just put me in autopilot, powering through the class to get a grade instead of to learn.

If you don't assume your students are acting with the best intentions, it can come at the price of a loss of trust, and even otherwise harmless or well-intentioned conversations can develop an emotional charge. When you give your students the benefit of the doubt by assuming the best of intentions, conversations immediately become much easier and far less complicated.

Action #2: Be Curious

When you assume the best of intentions, you avoid defensiveness and distrust, and are freed up to communicate, instead, with curiosity. You can ask questions without jumping to conclusions, minimizing a student's needs, or getting defensive. You can understand their perspective much better.

Understandably, people become defensive when they feel like they're being unfairly criticized. But if you combine assuming the best of intentions and interacting with others from a place of curiosity, even emotionally charged situations can be quickly diffused.

Picture yourself in an argument with your spouse. You spend an hour painstakingly laying out all the wrongs you've perceived, *very clearly,* and at the end, they look at you blankly.

"I still don't get why you're mad," they tell you.

Steam shoots out of your ears *Looney Tunes*–style, and you take the deepest breath of your life, because you're about to *explode*.

Imagine if instead, they responded with, "Can you tell me more about why you're feeling this way? I want to understand."

No shouting match, no bad vibes for the rest of the night—they're curiously seeking to understand, and you know they care about how you feel. There's connection there, where before there was only anger.

When people are defensive, there's very little chance of a productive outcome. But when you're curious, there's always an opening for one.

"I just want you to be happy..."

You've undoubtedly heard this before from someone in your life: "I just want you to be happy."

Many of our parents have said it to us. We say it to our spouses and our kids. But in my experience, I rarely hear anyone ask—from a Platinum perspective—the *obvious* next question: "What does happy mean to you?"

When I run up against a concept I'm curious about, diving deep into research is *my* happy place. Earlier in my career, I did a study where I asked 800 children, ages kindergarten to sixth grade, a question:

"What does happy mean to you?"

They could write or draw their answer, or both. The variety in the responses was striking. Some—many—were hilarious. One was: "Happy to me is playing outside with a group of friends and laugh ing together and telling private jokes." Another kid wrote: "Happy to me is playing video games by myself on my bed and my bed is made of gold."

Often, what we do to create happiness for other people is based on our own assumptions. Looking at these two children, I never would have known how radically different their ideas of happiness were.

Whenever I'm wondering something about someone or something, when I don't feel clear but I *think* I have an idea, I remember that fourth grader and his bed of gold. And I realize something: I actually don't know. I don't know at all. Luckily, though, I can almost always find out—by showing curiosity, and by listening to understand.

Action #3: Listen to Understand

This is the counterpart to Be Curious. Asking questions is überimportant—but how you listen is just as crucial.

The next time someone tells you what they think or how they feel, notice:

Are you listening to *understand?*

Or are you listening to decide if you agree or disagree?

Perhaps you're not really listening at all—you're internally formulating what you're going to say next.

If you can relate, hello and welcome; we've all been there. We listen to respond nearly automatically, and not because we're rude. Typically, it's because we're excited—we want to build on someone's comment, or it sparked a memory or new idea we want to share.

Listening to *understand* requires taking yourself out of the equation and focusing entirely on the other person. What they're saying is not about *you*. It's about them—what they think, what they feel, what they need.

So, pause. Digest what they're saying. You can tell you're listening to understand when every word the other person says inspires a new opportunity to understand them more deeply. Questions come to you that will help you connect; you're intrigued and driven to fully understand what they're communicating to you.

Asking follow-up questions that take the conversation deeper—and importantly, that keep it focused on *them*—lets the other person know that they're being truly heard. And when you're listening to understand, you might find that you need time to sit with their message before continuing the conversation. There's no rush to respond; understanding takes time.

Action #4: Use "I" Statements

What I hear you saying is...

From what I understand, you'd like to...

In communication, the only thing you know for sure is what you received. By communicating this using "I" statements like the above, you leave the assumptions off the table, out of the debate. You are owning your perspective.

"I" statements signal an openness that's critical to good communication. By using them, you show you understand that your perspective might be different from someone else's. Communicating what you received moves the conversation forward and eliminates confusion. Often, following up "I" statements with a question—"Is that right?" or "Am I understanding this correctly?"—can help, too, especially when a student isn't clear on why they're confused.

Action #5: Infuse Positivity

Remember that the classroom's mood and outlook begin with you. And research backs this up; a teacher's positive mindset makes a huge impression on the classroom environment.

Teachers who exhibit positive emotions build stronger relationships with their students.[12]

A teacher's positive emotions can "undo" the emotional and physiological effects of negative emotions and stress, creating an environment more conducive to learning.[13]

Teacher enthusiasm transfers to students and is a powerful predictor of

---

12 https://files.eric.ed.gov/fulltext/EJ1399789.pdf

13 https://www.jstor.org/stable/30189914

students' intrinsic motivation.[14]

Positive Psychology researcher Michelle Gielan asserts that the best time to infuse positivity is when you begin conversations. She calls this a Power Lead. "Nowhere is your power to meaningfully influence others more evident than at the start of an interaction," writes Michelle. "The way we start off conversations often predicts how they unfold."[15]

When starting a lesson or discussion in the classroom, get yourself into an optimistic mindset. Think about something that was fun or brought you joy, and share it. It will set the tone for the entire interaction—and positively impact the resulting thinking, perspectives, and outcomes of your students.

Recently, I had a busy day of meetings and the thought of what to make for dinner, once again, had taken a backseat. So, feeling a bit bedraggled, I hit the In-N-Out drive-thru with my two teenage boys. Our cashier, Madison (I'll never forget her name!), glanced curiously at the two boys in the car. As she handed me our delicious-smelling paper bags full of food, she mentioned offhand, "Wow, you look too young to have two kids that age!"

I melted. "I was not expecting that, and you have no idea how much I needed that! You made my night!" I gushed. Madison smiled hesitantly and shrunk back slightly into the drive-thru window, clearly wondering

---

14   Patrick, Brian C., Jennifer Hisley, and Toni Kempler. 2000. "'What's Everybody So Excited About?': The Effects of Teacher Enthusiasm on Student Intrinsic Motivation and Vitality." The Journal of Experimental Education 68 (3): 217–36. doi:10.1080/00220970009600093.

15   Michelle Gielan, "Power Lead Your Next Conversation," BetterUp, September 2, 2019, https://www.betterup.com/blog/power-lead-your-next-conversation.

what can of worms she'd accidentally opened with this harried, messy-ponytailed, emotionally unstable customer. Meanwhile, I drove off on cloud nine.

The next morning, I told a group I was working with about Madison's comment. I asked how their previous nights had gone. Sure enough, almost everyone shared a positive story, and we had one of our most productive, energetic sessions ever.

IS EVERYONE BEING HEARD?

Not every kid is outgoing and outspoken. Many are much happier letting their peers carry the conversation in the classroom.

To create a classroom culture built on great communication, all voices need space to be heard. Take a moment to think about the environment you foster in your classroom—are you making space for all those different voices?

Or are a few of the loudest ones taking up all the space?

Amplifying all voices is active, not passive. Instead of leaving it to each student to speak up, actively create opportunities for all voices. Ask the quieter students what they think. Bring up the insights a more timid student shared with you. Or just sit with the silence; often, the best nuggets of wisdom and connection lie in the moments of silence between the talking.

A great communication culture is one where every student is secure in the value of their contributions, and is certain that their teacher wants to hear and understand them. If you build it, they will speak. (Most of the time, anyway.)

In the case of Jordan's book analysis gone wrong, it didn't take long for Mr. Ellis to uncover what had happened. In fact, it was a simple issue that tended to crop up when students transferred from other schools, as Jordan had done: what Jordan had learned about analysis at his previous school simply didn't match the expectations at his new one.

Compounding the problem was the fact that Jordan *didn't know what he didn't know*. He couldn't explain why he couldn't follow the instructions, because he thought he *was* following them. He was doing what he thought "analysis" was. Then he'd get his work back, see the bad grade, and retreat further into himself, lost and confused.

With every assignment that missed the mark, the gap between him and his classmates widened—and his insecurity and embarrassment grew. The last thing Jordan was going to do in that emotional state was raise his hand in front of his peers to ask Mr. Ellis to explain what seemingly everyone else already knew.

COMMUNICATION = CONNECTION = SUCCESS

As Sam told us, he got to the root of the issue that day after class with Jordan. "When you say you wrote down what happened, that's the *summarize* part of the instructions. What does *analyze* mean to you?"

Jordan was clearly confused. "I thought summarize and analyze were the same thing."

"Ahh, got it. That's super helpful, Jordan," Mr. Ellis said, nodding. "I think I see where the disconnect happened. Let's go through Chapter 2 together, and I'll show you what I mean."

First, he asked Jordan to summarize the chapter. Jordan did so easily, recounting what the main character did. There was obviously no problem with reading comprehension.

"So, why do you think the character did that?" Mr. Ellis asked next.

Jordan didn't skip a beat. "Because of what happened earlier in the first chapter. He was mad because..." and he continued with a spot-on analysis of the character's emotional state, one that stacked up to what the top students in the class had handed in.

"And why do you think the author put that in there? What's she trying to say?"

Again, with no help whatsoever, Jordan rattled off a perfect analysis of the theme of the chapter—he even tossed in, unprompted, a few outside comparisons to Marvel movie plots and *Avatar: The Last Airbender* to strengthen his points.

Not only was Jordan *capable* of analysis, he was *good* at it. He appeared to enjoy it, even, his face lighting up as he connected the dots between characters and themes.

"I almost laughed aloud," Sam said to us in our roundtable later on. "Because here I thought I was working with this kid who was really struggling. Nope—there was just a ball dropped or a wire crossed somewhere before he came to my class on what "analysis" was. Once I told him it was basically just explaining the *why*, rather than the *what*, he had zero problems re-doing the project. And he knocked it out of the park on his second try, now that he finally understood what he was supposed to do."

Sam continued, "It really showed me how important it is to clarify that students don't just *hear* me, but that they *understand* me. It seems so obvious now that I think about it. I feel terrible that Jordan was struggling in silence for so long just because of a single misunderstood word."

Going forward, Sam made a habit of checking in with Jordan more frequently, asking clarifying questions and encouraging him to share his thoughts. And Jordan, in turn, felt more comfortable seeking help when he needed it. By the end of the semester, his grades had improved significantly, but more importantly, so had his confidence.

Looking back, Mr. Ellis realized how crucial it was to ensure that his instructions were truly understood. He'd assumed that his detailed explanations and handouts were enough, but Jordan's experience taught him otherwise. How many other students might be hearing something different from a word or phrase I assumed we all understood?

From then on, he made a point to ask his students, "How do you plan to approach this?" or "Can you explain the instructions in your own words?" Those small adjustments made a world of difference.

For Jordan, the experience was transformative. According to Sam, he went from a quiet, withdrawn kid to one who regularly spoke up in class to help connect the dots for other students.

"In fact, he's my go-to guy for pop culture references now," Sam told us on our next call. "Anytime the class is stuck on a particular subject, I make eye contact with Jordan and say, "Got anything for me?" He immediately rattles off the plot of half a dozen movies or TV shows or video games, and helps it click for everyone else. I thought this kid had serious reading comprehension issues—turns out he might be the next CEO of Netflix!"

CLASSROOM ACTION PLAN: UNDERSTAND THEIR UNDERSTANDING

1. Teach your students the types of feedback you provide and the reasons behind them.

2. Ask your students "What type of feedback do you like to receive?"

3. For a bellringer activity, have students write down their favorite way to demonstrate their learning.

Scan here for a downloadable action plan you can take into the classroom!

3

ALIGN

"Carmen, you're smart, talented, and creative. I know you can do even better."

Mrs. Sheridan prided herself on one thing above all else as a teacher: her unshakeable belief in her students, and her emphasis on telling them, constantly, exactly how much she believed in them.

With most of her students, this served to strengthen their relationship; the kids blossomed under the warmth of Mrs. Sheridan's belief in them.

With Carmen, a freshman in her class, it seemed to work the *opposite* way. The more Mrs. Sheridan expressed belief in Carmen, the more upset Carmen seemed to get.

She had to admit that it wasn't just Carmen, either. Mrs. Sheridan had begun to notice this reaction from certain students when she encouraged them and told them how much she believed in them. Mrs. Sheridan was relatively new to teaching, only in her second year—she'd started out convinced that if she just believed in her students, they'd believe in themselves, too. At first, it worked; when she encouraged them, they tried harder. When she praised them and invited them to stretch even further next time, they did just that. But as she got more experience under her belt, she noticed that it *didn't* work with all of them. Some of her students actually got *worse* when she encouraged them to go after their potential.

On a Spark roundtable, Christine Sheridan told us about Carmen, who was "*so* bright, *so* talented, but has possibly the lowest self-esteem I've ever seen in a kid. I build her up and act as her personal hype woman, but she is just not having it." She talked about how Carmen bristled at praise and rolled her eyes at encouragement. "Anything I say that calls out her potential is met with "whatever". She just doesn't want to hear it."

"How does she take feedback on her work?" Monica, who was leading the call for the Spark teachers, asked Christine.

"That's the odd thing—she takes it just fine. I'll point out something she did wrong, and she fixes it right away. She's not defensive or anything. It's like she's only defensive when I actually praise her!"

Christine had brought up Carmen on the call as an example of escalating behavior issues. The student had begun acting out more and more lately, making snarky comments under her breath when Christine gave the class instructions and rolling her eyes or sighing loudly when Christine talked about another student's achievements.

"Do you think she might be jealous?" Monica asked.

Christine chewed her lip for a moment, then said, "I honestly don't know. I don't see how she could be; I call out her achievements just as often. But for whatever reason, we are *not* on the same wavelength about how well she's doing and how much potential she has."

Some of the best turnarounds teachers talk about with Spark is in the realm of this chapter's subject, and Christine's issue with Carmen: *alignment.*

Ask yourself: are you sure you and your students are on the same page about what you expect from them?

NO CLARITY, NO RESULTS

Have you ever felt like you're speaking into a void, repeating yourself endlessly, and still not getting through to your students? You're not alone. Misaligned expectations—whether about classroom behavior, success criteria, or learning objectives—are one of the most common sources of frustration for teachers. When students don't fully understand what's expected of them, they often shut down, leaving teachers feeling stuck in a cycle of correction and clarification.

Misalignment often stems from a gap between what teachers think they're communicating and what students actually *hear* (as in, the lesson Sam from the previous chapter learned with his student Jordan). You might say, "Complete this quietly and turn it in when you're done," but a student who's distracted or unfamiliar with the routine might miss critical details. Similarly, if success criteria for a lesson are too vague—"Write a strong essay," for example—students may feel unsure about what's required. For example, you may have meant "strong" as in "backed by evidence", but they heard "strong" as in "use powerful quotes". They write what *they* think is "strong" and it misses the mark entirely. They get a bad grade, you're frustrated that they didn't listen to instructions, and they're utterly confused about where they went wrong. Worse, they internalize the misalignment, as young people often do, assuming that they *must* be the one in the wrong. And that means they must be stupid. And bad at school. And…you're probably familiar with how quickly that can spiral in a kid's mind.

In her book *The Skillful Teacher*, educator and researcher Robyn Jackson emphasizes that clear expectations are a cornerstone of effective teaching. When students know exactly what's expected, they're more likely to stay motivated and less likely to exhibit off-task behaviors. In contrast, unclear or inconsistent expectations create anxiety and confusion, which can lead to shutdowns or even outright resistance.

When students know exactly what is expected of them, it's like a sigh of relief. *I'm not going to mess up. I know exactly what I'm aiming for.*

Deep down, the overwhelming majority of students really want to succeed. They want to do their best. They want to pull their weight, they want to contribute, and they want to perform. Without clearly delineated expectations from their teacher, students have no way of knowing what success looks like; they're essentially flying blind.

Success, like everything else, is a matter of perspective. Without a teacher who clearly states what they're looking for, students are left to determine what success looks like via their own perspective and background of experience. They might draw their perspective of success from previous teachers. On a fundamental level, expectations diverge in ways neither party is aware of.

This can lead to incredible frustration and ultimately prevent students from connecting with their teachers. When someone is working hard to succeed, but continually told they're missing the mark—or even when they're doing great, but that performance is rarely called out and celebrated—it can be demoralizing. They may feel like they're unable to do their best, that their efforts are invalidated. *What's the point in trying?* This is a quick road to student disengagement; and with disengagement comes vastly reduced performance. You've probably seen what it looks like when a kid is just *checked out*. They're going nowhere fast.

STUDENTS SPEAK

"For me, it's really hard to want to wake up and go to school if I don't actively have something I'm trying to work toward. That's why Spark was nice—because at the beginning of the week, or for the day, or even the month, you set three goals. It helped me progressively work toward those goals, come in every day, and stay focused."

Research consistently demonstrates a strong link between student engagement and academic performance. Disengaged students often exhibit poorer academic outcomes, including lower grades, increased absenteeism, and higher dropout rates.

A study published in the *European Journal of Psychology of Education* examined student engagement patterns and their relationship to academic self-concept and achievement. The researchers found that students who actively participated and were cognitively and emotionally engaged in learning activities achieved higher academic success. Conversely, disengaged students, characterized by minimal participation and lack of emotional investment, demonstrated lower academic achievement.[16]

A disengaged student is at a standstill when it comes to performance. Forget brilliance—any spark at all is going to fizzle right out.

EXPECTATIONS + CLARITY = CONFIDENCE

Carmen's behavior got more and more disruptive as the weeks went on. It was clear she was frustrated—but at what?

She began arguing with Christine over simple instructions, challenging every correction. Day by day, the classroom became a battleground. Carmen's snarky remarks grew louder. Finally, one day, she accidentally knocked over her chair while standing to argue a point about why the math problem didn't "matter anyway." The chair made a huge racket, bouncing and clattering across the concrete floor. Christine felt Carmen's emotional contagion vibrate through the rest of the kids in the room—frustration, anger, resentment—and knew class was effectively over for the day, even if she had these students for forty-five more minutes.

She also knew, based on the embarrassed look on Carmen's face, that it wasn't that Carmen *wanted* to disrupt the class—not really. She just didn't know where else to put the overwhelming sense of failure that seemed to follow her around, and she was taking it out on Christine.

Once the bell rang, Christine asked Carmen to stay behind. The rest of the class filtered out, tension radiating out into the hallway. Carmen looked

16 Schnitzler, K., Holzberger, D. & Seidel, T. All better than being disengaged: Student engagement patterns and their relations to academic self-concept and achievement. Eur J Psychol Educ 36, 627–652 (2021). https://doi.org/10.1007/s10212-020-00500-6

defeated and slightly frightened.

"Talk to me," Christine said. "What was that all about?"

It took a solid ten minutes of breaking through Carmen's initial defensiveness to uncover a platinum nugget.

"Why should I even try, if nothing is ever good enough for you?" Carmen eventually said.

Christine was taken aback. "For the life of me, I could *not* figure out where she got that idea," she told us later on our roundtable call. "I feel like all I do is tell the kids how much I believe in them and how great I know they can be."

But something in what Carmen said also sparked Christine's curiosity—something that had been brought out even more intensely in our Spark roundtables, where we work on responding to feeling defensive or confused with kind, clarifying questions.

"Why do you think nothing is ever good enough for me?" she asked.

"Because you say so. All the time. Even when I do good, all you say is "do better"."

Christine opened her mouth and took a breath to say *No I don't*—and then stopped. Because, as she suddenly realized to her horror, that was *exactly* what she had been saying.

"I was telling kids, "I believe in you. I know you can be great. I know you can do even better,"" Christine told us in our roundtable. "And for a lot of them, this felt great. It motivated them knowing I was cheering them on. But for students like Carmen who are perfectionists, all they heard was that they weren't great *yet*. They weren't perfect *yet*. "You can do better" meant "you didn't hit the mark this time. This isn't good enough. *You're* not good enough.""

Christine shook her head. "Call it a newbie mistake, call it me being too naive, or even call it me forgetting the Platinum Rule—but that was an intense moment for me. I realized that to some of these kids, belief feels like *expectations*. And my expectations weren't clear."

ALIGNMENT ACTION PLAN

When expectations are clear and aligned, it's like flipping a switch. Suddenly, the fog lifts, and both teachers and students can focus on what really matters: learning and growth. Research shows that clarity in communication and expectations is one of the most effective ways to foster student engagement and success; in fact, a comprehensive review in *Frontiers in Psychology* defines teacher clarity as one of the most important indicators of student success.[17]

As the teacher, alignment begins with you. Here are some key actions you can take today that will get you there with your students.

Action #1: Clarity Is Kind

Everyone wants to succeed, but precisely *no one* wants to fly blind at a

---

17 https://www.frontiersin.org/journals/psychology/articles/10.3389/fpsyg.2021.712419/full

target that's hidden in the clouds. When faced with an unclear idea of what success looks like, most people—adults included—disengage. They stop trying. Why bother, when they don't know if their efforts will actually get them where they want to?

Clarity is kind, and it builds trust in the classroom like almost nothing else. As the teacher, it's your job to provide clear, specific criteria for what success looks like. A lot of the time, this is best communicated with an example of completed work that meets your expectations. Show them the target, talk about how they'll get there, and watch them go after it with confidence.

Action #2: Spend Time in the Present

Tell me if this sounds familiar: as a teacher, you set a reach goal for your students that you feel is just aspirational enough to motivate them toward greater potential. Yet when you try to pump them up about the goal, they stare back at you blankly, totally nonplussed.

Goals that seem completely unrealistic are actually *demotivating*. And, as Christine discovered with Carmen, constantly focusing on where Carmen could go next only served to make Carmen feel like she wasn't good enough *right now*.

Education is about growth, forward progress, and preparing for the future. But that doesn't mean you need to make the future your sole focus. Spent time in the present with students, meeting and celebrating them exactly where they are. If you take that time, you can check in to be sure you're on the same page with them before you move on to what's expected of them next.

Action #3: Order of Priority

Recall what we discussed earlier: most students, deep down, want to succeed. They want to perform. Effective prioritizing, however, rarely comes naturally to kids, so it often looks like attacking an assignment or project like the never-ending pasta bowl at Olive Garden. The best teachers understand that most students need to be taught not just what their work *is*, but how to approach and knock out that work.

Once you've gotten clear on the details and given the context for your expectations, ask your students for their plan to tackle the goal. Share your insights and direction so that they end up with a clear order and priority they should stick with. In these discussions, it's also important to align on everything else they currently have on their plates. Their existing priorities from other teachers, activities, and their families are just as important to the equation as the new ones you're giving them. Take the time to discuss and mutually agree on a plan for how they're going to get things done. From there, they have a clear runway to take off.

Action #4: Context is Key

Tell me if this sounds familiar: you introduce a new concept or project to your class, something you believe will challenge and inspire them to grow. You're excited about the possibilities, and you've been prepping the lesson for weeks.

But when you introduce it to them, you're met with blank stares and half-hearted nods. The energy in the room fizzles. They are decidedly—as the kids themselves would say—not into it.

Ask yourself: do they know why they should be excited about it?

If you asked them, "Why does this matter? Why am I asking you to do this?", would they know the answer?

Goals or tasks that feel disconnected or overwhelming can be demotivating for students. You can shift their perspective by giving them the why behind what they're learning. When students understand not just what they're doing but why it matters, they're far more likely to engage and invest in the process. Context transforms abstract or challenging material into something tangible and meaningful. It helps students see themselves as active participants in their learning journey, not just passive recipients of information.

Imagine a teacher who assigns a complex research project on water quality. Without context, students might see it as just another assignment to check off. But if the teacher explains how this project connects to real-world issues—like how their findings could inspire local community action or influence school policies—suddenly, the work feels relevant and impactful. Students begin to see themselves as contributors to their community, not just students completing a task.

The same thing goes for smaller, day-to-day lessons. The math formulas they're wrestling with aren't just numbers on a page; they're tools to be used for everything from personal finance to building bridges. Compound interest is a lot more engaging for students when they see how quickly their money can multiply when invested in a retirement fund.

By giving students context, you're not just teaching them facts or skills—you're helping them see the value in what they're learning. You're showing them how their efforts contribute to their growth and the world around them. This is bolstered by recent research by John Hattie, who found in *Visible Learning: Mathematics, Grades K-12* that math instruction is most effective when it moves beyond rote memorization and instead promotes conceptual understanding and problem-solving through real-world examples. Give a kid the why behind what they're learning—and how it's going to affect them in the future—and you'll be able to keep their attention and make the lesson stick.

SPARK STUDY RESULTS

In our independent Spark study, student growth scores shot through the roof at the Spark school. Here are the middle school results:

- In Grade 6, students at the Spark school showed 29.71 points higher growth. (Wow!)

- In Grade 7, students at the Spark school showed 6.81 points higher growth.

- In Grade 8, students at the Spark school showed 13.36 points higher growth.

EXPECTING BRILLIANCE

Christine's moment of clarity with Carmen forced her to sit down and seriously examine how she was communicating her expectations to students.

"I realized that a lot of where I was coming from was my own stuff from when I was a kid," she admitted. "I never felt like anyone believed in me when I was younger. If just one person had said to me, "You can do it, Christine, I believe in you," I really think it would have completely changed how I showed up to school and how much I liked it. And it would have changed the opportunities I saw for myself."

A lot of her students *were* like her, and that's why her cheerleading had worked for them. But in stopping there, Christine was stuck in the Golden Rule. To reach students like Carmen, she had to go Platinum.

"I asked myself, *if belief feels like expectations to some students, then how can I make those expectations ultra-clear?* Because I do really feel strongly about showing students how much I believe in them. But I could make it clearer what I actually believed they were capable of *doing*."

Which is exactly what she did with Carmen. That day in her one-on-one, Christine took a step back from focusing so much on the future. Instead, she focused on the past. She showed Carmen how far she'd come already that year, how much better her performance was with each assignment the student turned in.

"I'm seeing you do two or three times better than your last work every time you turn something in," Christine explained. "So I'm not just making it up that you're going to do better next time. I know that you will, because *you already did*. That doesn't mean you didn't meet expectations. It actually means you keep *beating* my expectations."

Carmen looked calmer, but still unconvinced. "But you still want me to do better."

Christine shook her head. "I want you to keep doing great, because I believe you can. Here's an example. You play soccer, right?" Christine said. She already knew the answer. Carmen didn't just *play*; she'd made the varsity team as a freshman. "When you win a game, what do you all do to celebrate?"

Carmen described pizza, locker room chants, and a few other rituals. "And then you stop practicing, right? Because you already won, so you're done. You can't do better," Christine continued.

Carmen scoffed. "Mrs. G, of course not. We can always do better."

It took a moment, but then understanding dawned on Carmen's face. *"Oh."*

"Your work in the classroom is just like that," Christine said. "You're already great. You already won! But there's no such thing as perfect. You'll never be done; you just keep getting better and better." She paused and noticed how Carmen's tense body language had relaxed somewhat—but not all the way. "I get that me telling you to do better isn't a good target. You need a clear goal. Would it help if I gave you a really specific goal on each assignment to shoot for, and that's what you focus on winning?"

Carmen nodded eagerly.

"It's not going to be easy," Christine warned her. "You're going to have to still work really hard to hit the goal."

"Yeah, but at least I know where the goal is!"

Christine tried not to wince. *Can't fault her for honesty, that's for sure.*

That day marked a huge shift in how Christine approached expectations with her students. "I realized that believing in them is incredibly important, and always will be," she told us. "But helping them actually get wins is even more important, because that's what builds their confidence and belief in *themselves*."

As an educator, you hold the keys to your students' performance.

Aligned expectations feel like flow. Everyone is clear, motivated, and moving in the same direction. Performance soars; students feel like they're doing their best, and their potential blossoms visibly. You'll see them spark in ways you hadn't anticipated. Remember—*they want to perform.* They just need you to clearly lay out what good performance means to you, show them where they've already succeeded, and determine a structure of priorities that sets them up for a win.

At the heart of aligning on expectations is the Platinum Rule. Individually, with each student, get on the same page when it comes to both of your perspectives on the goals, details, and priorities of their work. What they share might surprise you—and, like Christine, help you reach the next level of your own teaching journey.

CLASSROOM ACTION PLAN: ALIGN ON EXPECTATIONS

1. Create a T-chart with your students. On one side, ask what is the teacher's role in a student's education. On the other side, have students define their own role in their learning.

2. Facilitate a class discussion about what happens when someone does not fulfill their role.

3. Once completed, display the T-chart on the classroom wall and have students commit to upholding their responsibilities by signing it.

Scan here for a downloadable action plan you can take into the classroom!

4

CONNECT

When I ask teachers, "What is the hardest thing you've ever had to face in your career?", a huge percentage of them reply with a single word.

COVID.

"*So* stressful. *So* hard. How do you hold their attention through a computer screen for hours on end? How do you make them care? How do you build a *relationship?*"

The pandemic wasn't just felt acutely by teachers; I coached dozens of corporate leaders during that time who were beside themselves trying to hold their companies together. Teams fell apart; employees disengaged. The biggest learning curve was also one that took our internet-obsessed, global population by somewhat of a surprise: despite all of us being accustomed to the carefully curated veneer of social media, it turns out that *authenticity* is absolutely crucial for real connection.

And authenticity through a carefully-curated Zoom window is about as easily achieved as naming every member of BTS without resorting to Google. ("Who on earth is BTS", you're saying? I feel you.)

One of our Spark teachers, Maura, is a spectacular storyteller, delivering details in a hilariously dry, deadpan tone. When asked about when she most struggled with authenticity in the classroom, she regaled us for nearly a half hour with her personal pandemic tale of woe (one that every other teacher on the call, I later learned, identified with *bigtime*).

"Even after ten years of teaching, I was always a little self-conscious about my classroom style," she began. Her students were polite and respectful, but they didn't open up to her the way they did with other teachers. She envied her colleagues, who always seemed to know which students were into anime or football or obscure indie bands. Other classrooms buzzed with energy and laughter, while hers felt sterile in comparison. "I told myself I was just a different kind of teacher—more serious, more structured—but deep down, I didn't feel like I could be authentic with them, and I knew they felt the same way about me."

At a professional development workshop, a speaker talked about the importance of authenticity in building trust with students. "You don't have to be their friend," the speaker said, "but you *do* have to let them see the real you. Authenticity is about showing up as yourself and meeting them where they are." Maura took this to heart, and decided to start small. At the beginning of each class, she tried sharing a little bit about herself. Nothing too personal—just anecdotes about her weekend or the book she was reading. It felt awkward at first, like she was performing a monologue for a reluctant audience. But over time, the students began to respond. They asked follow-up questions or shared their own stories. "You like hiking, Mrs. Carter? Have you ever been to Castlewood Canyon?" one student asked, and a lively conversation about favorite trails followed.

She also started paying closer attention to the details her students shared, jotting down notes to help her remember. When Marcus mentioned his soccer tournament, she asked him about it the following week. When Lily talked about her art portfolio, Maura made a point to ask if she'd entered any competitions. "The small moments added up. The classroom started to feel different. I let myself, for one brief, shining moment, feel like I was winning the authenticity battle, breaking through to the next level of my skill as a teacher."

And then the pandemic hit.

Like most schools across the world, the classroom was forced into an abrupt shift to remote learning, and suddenly, everything Maura had worked so hard to build felt like it was slipping through her fingers.

"The first week of online classes was a disaster. *A disaster*. Half the students didn't turn on their cameras," she told us. Those who did often looked distracted or bored—if their cameras were even pointing at their faces (the kids figured out pretty quick how to aim it so just the tops of their heads were in the frame). Her attempts at lighthearted banter fell flat, met with awkward silences or stilted one-word replies.

"It was a tough pill to swallow, realizing that I relied so much on being in the same room with the kids to form connections," she said. "With the computer screen between us, it's like everything I'd been practicing in my old playbook went out the window. It was impossible to read their energy. I couldn't overhear their chitchat to remember personal details—I only saw them on scheduled Zoom calls. Even though we all lived in the same city, those kids felt like they were a million miles away."

Maura was missing the one ingredient that she'd worked so hard on—and that was so incredibly difficult to achieve through a screen. If she wanted to stay connected to her students, she had to figure out how to bring the *authenticity* back into the online classroom.

BE SEEN, BE KNOWN, BELONG

Quick question before we continue:

What's your *Harry Potter* house? Gryffindor, Ravenclaw, Hufflepuff, Slytherin?

I'd be willing to bet that most of you reading this book know exactly what your house is, because over the past couple of decades, you've likely taken—or at least seen, or been sent by a friend—any one of the countless online quizzes that place you in your Hogwarts house based on your personality traits. (And in case it isn't abundantly clear so far in how much I've talked about loving school and studying, I'm a Ravenclaw.)

Okay, maybe you've never taken that particular quiz. So, next question: which character from *Friends* are you?

Or, which Marvel Avenger—or villain—are you most like?

Or, what breed of dog are you?

I'd be hard pressed to count all the silly, fun online quizzes I've taken over the years—everything from which breakfast food best represents my personality (chocolate croissant) to which decade I was meant to live in (clearly the 80s, for anyone who knows me well).

Why do we love online quizzes?

As fun as they are, and as much as we all know they don't hold much meaning—they still make us feel seen. They make us feel *known*.

I need to take a little responsibility here. Because if you've been inundated over the course of your internet lifetime with dozens of random quizzes your friends tag you on, or that pop up in your social feeds… well, I'm one of the people you have to thank for that. (You're welcome. Or, sorry.)

Back in my mid-twenties, when I'd just finished grad school, a couple of fellow grads from Harvard Business School approached me to join their new startup, Emode. Emode was built on the concept that insights into human psychology and behavior could be freely collected online through quizzes—and the feedback would create a system for understanding human motivation. These insights could be applied to product development and marketing, helping new products go viral.

At the time, this idea was groundbreaking, and as a student of cognitive psychology, I eagerly jumped at the opportunity to help shape a system for collecting data on human behavior and motivations. I became Emode's Head of Content Development. I had no idea what I was doing yet, but neither did any of us; we were just a bunch of kids in a basement in Cambridge (one of whom was *the* Mel Robbins).

Our team created and launched little quizzes and personality tests that were similar to, at the time, the kind of thing you'd see in *Cosmopolitan* magazine—but applying more research and psychology to drive a real insightful result, rather than just offer entertainment. The quizzes were fun, often pop-culture-oriented, and highly shareable (but this was *long* before social media, so pasting the link into email was the most popular way they would be shared).

The very first quiz I created was "What Breed of Dog Are You?" I based the quiz questions and scoring on personality research, dog research, and anything else I thought would tease out the kind of results we were looking for: people giving input on their deepest likes, dislikes, behavior, and motivations.

When we put that first quiz on the internet, we had no expectation whatsoever of how much attention it would get.

To our utter shock, people went *nuts*.

It spread like wildfire. Within a few weeks, the link to our quiz was—no exaggeration—the most widely clicked link in the entire world.

"What Breed of Dog Are You?" ultimately settled to a daily unique visit rate of one million visitors per *day*. For 1999, this was like winning ten Super Bowls. It was completely unprecedented. The *New York Times* wrote an article about the popularity of the quiz. We got tons of media attention. And before long, lo and behold—a Bay Area venture capital firm came calling. Emode scored first-round funding, became Tickle. com, and a handful of us moved out to San Francisco.

I went on to write nearly one hundred quizzes for Tickle.com. Each one dug in deeper and deeper to how people truly thought about themselves and how they understood and perceived their inner world. It was the ultimate continuation of what I had learned in Dr. Duckworth's class: understanding somebody else's understanding, so that you know how they want to be treated. The quizzes were essentially a Platinum Rule vehicle.

It was work that I loved. No matter how fun or frothy the subject of a quiz was, it still represented a moment for someone to sit down, self-reflect, and understand themselves better—even if all they thought they were doing was having fun. I was deeply fulfilled by bringing that opportunity to people. So deeply fulfilled, in fact, that I knew I wanted it to be the basis of my career: helping people find self-awareness.

All the insights we learned through the quizzes we delivered coalesced into one prevailing theme: people *love* learning about themselves. What's more, they love validating things they suspect about themselves. They love the feeling of being seen, known, and understood.

Sharing what seems like a silly quiz result actually feels like sharing a piece of themselves. It's a way of saying to the world: *I want to know me, and I want you to know me. I want you to understand my understanding. Here are new words, symbols, and avatars we can share to understand each other better.*

At its root, this sharing represents connection. People want to be known—because being known opens up the opportunity to *belong*.

BEYOND "REAL"

Teaching is one of the most relationship-intensive professions there is. Unlike a corporate team, where you're managing relationships with a small, consistent group of five to ten colleagues, teachers often have to connect authentically with dozens—sometimes hundreds—of students every year. In some cases, those connections must be built and sustained over the course of a single trimester or quarter. That's a daunting task, even for the most passionate and skilled educators.

It's easy to assume that the key to these relationships lies in authenticity.

After all, if teachers are "real" and show up as themselves, their students should naturally respond to that, right? Not quite. Authenticity is crucial, but it's not enough on its own. The ability to authentically connect with students isn't a matter of personality; it's about having the right tools in your toolkit. And it's absolutely crucial to develop those tools; in John Hattie's *Visible Learning for Teachers*, he found that "teacher credibility" had *twice* the impact on student outcomes as student motivation itself. "Teacher credibility" has a simple definition: it's the students' belief that they can learn from a teacher, based on trust, competence, dynamism, and immediacy.

I've spent time observing brilliant teachers—those rare individuals who seem to have an almost magical ability to connect with their students (both of my boys have been blessed to have had a few of these trajectory-changing teachers). What's fascinating is that these teachers don't all share the same personality type. One may be warm and extroverted, while another is quieter and more reserved. Yet the common thread is that they all excel at building meaningful relationships with their students.

On the flip side, I've also observed teachers with similar personalities who struggle to connect. It's not that they aren't authentic; they genuinely care about their students and bring their true selves into the classroom. The difference lies in their ability to draw on specific tools and strategies to create connection.

This brings us to a critical question: what makes students "like" a teacher? Rita Pierson, in her widely celebrated TED Talk *Every Kid Needs a Champion,* famously stated that "kids don't learn from people they don't like." But "liking" a teacher isn't about being fun or entertaining—it's about trust, respect, and feeling valued. In fact, feeling respected by their teacher can improve student performance, a recent Stanford study showed:

> A short, encouraging note on a highly marked-up essay could change the way students considered their teachers' critiques. Adding a note saying, "I'm giving you these comments because I have high standards and I know you can reach them," significantly boosted students' willingness to rewrite the paper: from 62 percent to 87 percent for white students, and from 17 percent to 71 percent of black students.[18]

Great relationships make us happier and help us perform better. On a deeper level, though, they help us thrive as humans.

Research shows that the greatest predictor of our happiness and long-term success as humans is the relationships we build. This is supported by The Harvard Study of Adult Development[19] that focuses on happiness and what predicts it. Incredibly, this study has been going on for more than eighty years, and in that time, it has found that social bonds not only predict overall happiness, health, and longevity, but also play a role in our career achievements, occupational success, and income.

Good relationships—deep, authentic bonds—don't just protect the body; they also protect the brain and spirit. This was evident to researchers again and again over the years as they interviewed participants, took blood tests, and tracked everything from marriage and divorce to jobs, careers, and illness. The consistent finding was that your background,

---

18 https://www.pbs.org/newshour/education/feeling-respected-transforms-student-school

19 Matthew Solan, "The Secret to Happiness? Here's Some Advice from the Longest-Running Study on Happiness," Harvard Health Publishing, October 5, 2017, https://www.health.harvard.edu/blog/the-secret-to-happiness-heres-some-advice-from-the-longest-running-study-on-happiness-2017100512543.

origin, or opportunities—the hand of cards you were dealt in life—had far less of an impact on your overall happiness than the quality of your relationships. Relationship quality has even been positively correlated with how long you live, how successful you feel, and how much money you make over the course of your career.

Let's talk about oxytocin—aka the "bonding hormone." It's the stuff that helps us feel connected, builds trust, and makes relationships thrive. You've probably heard about oxytocin when it comes to parent-child bonds or romantic relationships, but it also plays a big role in the classroom.

When teachers and students have meaningful, positive interactions, oxytocin gets released, and that hormone does some serious magic. It creates a sense of safety, trust, and connection. Think about it—when you feel like someone really sees you, believes in you, and has your back, doesn't that change everything? That's what oxytocin is doing behind the scenes for students, helping build those connections that are so critical for learning.

Research backs this up. A study in *Trends in Cognitive Sciences* shows that oxytocin helps us trust each other and strengthens emotional bonds. In the classroom, this means when you show kindness, empathy, or even just greet your students warmly, you're not just being nice—you're creating a space where they feel safe to take risks and engage. So, every time you acknowledge a student's effort, share a laugh, or offer encouragement, you're deepening that connection and reinforcing their trust in you.

Building these bonds doesn't have to be complicated. It's in the little things—like greeting students at the door, showing you care when they're struggling, or celebrating their wins.

Monica often shares an example of a certain teacher she worked with in the past who every day, without fail, stands at the door of his classroom before class and greets each student individually as they arrive. "I'm happy you're here," he tells them.

"It seems like the smallest thing," she says. "But that personal connection, that moment of acknowledgment, probably goes farther toward crafting the students' mindsets than almost anything else. They feel seen, they feel respected, and they feel like they belong."

Your job as a teacher is to craft authentic connections with your students. When a student has a positive relationship with their teacher, their motivation and performance increase. Strongly bonded, authentic relationships with your students will allow you to discover and focus on their strengths, spot and celebrate wins, provide meaningful feedback, and listen to understand.

Teaching *is* connection.

Approaching connection the right way is crucial. Done right, it's one of the most powerful tools in your educator toolkit. Done wrong, though, it only serves to reinforce the walls students build around themselves— walls that keep them feeling protected, but also make communication and collaboration that much more challenging.

The key differentiator between approaching connection the *right way* and *wrong way* is authenticity.

Authenticity can't be manufactured. It can't be fabricated. By definition, it's organic; it has to come from you naturally.

Authenticity arises from the deep-down desire to truly know and be known by others.

AUTHENTIC...WITH GUARDRAILS

New teachers often enter the classroom with the best intentions—a determination to connect with students, inspire learning, and maybe even change the world one kid at a time. But there's also a common pitfall for teachers just starting out: trying to be their students' *friend* more than just their teacher.

What happens when teachers try to be friends first? It's simple: they establish relationships that aren't rooted in structure. Students might test limits, skip assignments, or show up late because the foundation of respect and accountability hasn't been laid. And when the teacher eventually tries to enforce boundaries, it can feel like a betrayal to the students. "I thought we were cool! What do you mean, I can't have extra credit?"

The relationship between a teacher and a student is unique, and the connection formed in that space should reflect its specific dynamic. Think of it like any professional relationship. In a workplace, you wouldn't share every detail of your personal life with your colleagues. That doesn't mean you're being inauthentic—it just means you're respecting the boundaries of that relationship. The same principle applies in the classroom. Being authentic as a teacher doesn't require oversharing; it requires *intentional* sharing. It's about knowing what's appropriate to build trust and connection while maintaining the structure and purpose of the teacher-student dynamic.

Monica once told me a story about a teacher she'd worked with who blurred the teacher-student line disastrously. "Many mornings—I am not exaggerating—this teacher would roll into the school parking lot 20 to 30 minutes after the first bell had rung, first-period students left waiting in his classroom. And he would have two or three students in the car with him, iced coffees in hand. They'd all just come from a Dutch Bros run."

In the teacher's mind, he was doing something good—something noble, even. "These kids have never been to Dutch Bros before," he said when Monica brought it up, defending his actions. "No one's ever done this for them. I want to be that person." He saw himself as the *cool* teacher, the one who could give his students experiences they'd never had before.

When Monica told me this story the first time, all I could picture was Amy Poehler in *Mean Girls:* "I'm not like a regular mom. I'm a *cool mom.*" There's a reason that character was played for laughs—and made most parents watching cringe.

But in this teacher's mind, taking kids on coffee runs before school made him authentic and relatable. To put it politely, Monica saw it differently. "It's wildly inappropriate on so many levels," she told me. First, there was the blatant disregard for the students left waiting in the classroom while their teacher prioritized a coffee run. Then there was the undermining of what education was supposed to stand for: structure, accountability, and the importance of showing up prepared to learn. Finally, there was the obvious favoritism on display, which planted a seed of resentment among the students left behind.

You're an educator, so you can probably guess what ended up happening, right?

Yup, you got it: it backfired spectacularly. Starting off the school year with coffee runs meant that the teacher was wrapping up the semester with a bunch of undisciplined, resentful students who didn't get why they had to show up on time, do work on time, or take absolutely anything in school seriously.

Looking back, Monica saw this as a textbook example of good intentions gone wrong. The teacher had wanted to connect with his students, to show them care and kindness. But in doing so, he had crossed professional boundaries and lost sight of what his role as an educator was truly about. Authenticity in teaching isn't about being "cool" or bending the rules to win students over. It's about building trust and connection within the framework of respect and accountability.

I've heard Monica share this story with new teachers as a cautionary tale. "Your job is to guide and inspire," she'd say. "Not to be their best friend. There's a line, and when you cross it, you're not helping them anymore. You're hurting them."

AVOIDING AUTHENTICITY PITFALLS

So, Step 1 to authentic connection in the classroom: leave the Dutch Bros out of it. (I know, you're furiously underlining and highlighting this shocking revelation.)

But obvious blunders aside, that doesn't change the trickiness of authentic connection in the classroom. There are very real speedbumps nearly every teacher runs into when trying to build authenticity. If you're newer to your career, here are a few missteps to avoid (and if you're a seasoned educator, this could be a great list to review with your newer colleagues).

- **Trying to Be Friends First:** Students need a teacher, not another peer. Leading with friendship instead of structure can undermine respect.

- **Being Too Lenient Early On:** It's tempting to let small things slide at the beginning of the year—you don't want to be too harsh off the bat, right? But this sets a precedent that's hard to undo. Set boundaries from the beginning, explain the *why* behind them, and hold them firmly.

- **Overcompensating to Be Liked:** Being liked is a natural desire, but it's not the same as being respected. Respect comes from consistency and fairness.

Establishing boundaries early doesn't mean you can't connect with your students. In fact, it's the opposite. Boundaries create the space for authentic relationships to flourish. Once students respect the classroom and their teacher, they're more willing to engage, open up, and take risks in their learning. That's when the real magic happens.

Great teaching isn't about being the coolest or the strictest person in the room. It's about being a leader who sets the stage for students to feel safe, challenged, and inspired. An authentic teacher-student relationship is built on mutual respect and understanding. Here's what that might look like:

- **Keep It Relevant:** Share stories or insights that connect to the lesson or that help illustrate a concept. For example, if you're teaching about overcoming challenges, a brief story about a time you struggled with something and how you worked through it can be powerful.

- **Show Your Humanity:** It's okay to let students see that you're a real person with feelings and experiences. Sharing moments of vulnerability—like admitting when you've made a mistake—can help humanize you in their eyes.

- **Be Consistent:** Authenticity isn't just about what you share; it's about showing up with integrity every day. Students need to know they can rely on you to be fair, honest, and trustworthy.

- **Model Respect:** Treat your students with the same respect you expect from them. This mutual respect forms the foundation of any authentic relationship.

STUDENTS SPEAK

"I think once you open up more with your peers, you realize you have similarities, and that's where the real bond starts to form. You start to find commonalities you didn't know you had, and from there, it just spirals in a good way."

AN AUTHENTIC NEW NORMAL

Building authentic connection isn't always easy when you're working with dozens of students at a time. Even teachers who are great natural connectors often experience uncertainty when replicating the natural, easy relationships they have with individual students across an entire classroom. And authentic connections become an even *bigger* challenge when you're not able to physically be in the same room as the people you're trying to connect with.

Like, say, when your entire school day gets shrunk down to the size of your computer screen, and the students you're trying to connect with are blurry, often blank, video boxes. After her first week of online teaching during lockdown, Maura realized she needed a new approach. Her students were navigating an entirely new world, just like she was, and expecting them to engage the same way they had in person wasn't fair.

"I asked myself, "What do *they* need from me right now?"" she told us. The platinum answer, she realized, was patience, understanding, and a willingness to meet them where they were—even if that meant stepping out of her comfort zone.

The next day, Maura started class by asking her students how they were doing. "Not just "good" or "fine,"" she said. "I know we're all getting used to a new normal. Tell me one thing that's been hard this week and one thing that's been good." At first, only a few students responded, but as the weeks went on, more of them opened up.

She also made an effort to bring more creativity into her lessons. Instead of assigning a traditional essay, she asked her students to create video journals reflecting on how the pandemic was affecting them. The results surprised her. Even the quieter students shared candid, thoughtful reflections. One student talked about missing his grandmother, another about the stress of helping younger siblings with their homework while their parents worked long hours.

Maura responded to each video with personalized feedback, thanking her students for their honesty and sharing her own experiences when appropriate. "I really miss my mom too," she wrote to one student. "It's been hard not being able to visit her, but I'm trying to focus on the little things, like our weekly phone calls."

Slowly but surely, the connection she thought she'd lost began to return. It looked different than before, but it was no less meaningful.

"By the end of that semester, I'd realized something important: authenticity has *nothing* to do with whether we do lessons in person or on Zoom," Maura told us. "I thought I needed to keep things more focused on the lessons to combat the weird disconnect of the computer screen. But, as it turned out, acknowledging the discomfort we were all dealing with and leaning into it with humanity was what ended up connecting us all as we got used to things in the new normal."

As the classroom leader, the authenticity that will unite your students begins with you—and getting it right will create a classroom culture of trust and connection. Students are more likely to take risks, ask questions, and collaborate when they know their teacher is committed to building a real relationship with them.

Ask yourself: what makes you *you?* And how can you show that to your students, while also holding the boundaries so critical to respect and accountability?

Answering these questions is the beginning of a long investment, one that yields huge returns in true connection, and ultimately, a brilliantly connected, brilliantly performing classroom.

CLASSROOM ACTION PLAN: AUTHENTICALLY CONNECT

1. Learn each students' name as quickly as possible and use it correctly and intentionally.

2. Be mindful of your own emotional contagion and how it affects your students. Greet them at the door with that awareness .

3. Keep a chart with personal details about each student that you've learned over time. Refer to it regularly to strengthen relationships. For example, ask Willie about last week's football game every Monday or check in with Brodie about upcoming concerts he's excited for.

Scan here for a downloadable action plan you can take into the classroom!

5

BRILLIANCE

"Hey, Olivia, congratulations! I heard you made the basketball team! That's awesome."

Mr. Wilson, an eighth-grade ELA teacher, expected to see his student Olivia light up in response. He knew she'd been putting in a huge amount of time and effort after school to prep for tryouts for a top-level travel team. Olivia's older sister, Marina, was already a star player on the Varsity team at the local high school. Olivia had made the ultra-competitive travel team after just one year in the sport, which was a huge accomplishment—it showed the talent ran in the family.

To his confusion, Olivia shrugged nonchalantly. "Yeah," she said. "It's cool."

"I had never seen a kid's face match the words coming out of their mouth *less*," Jack Wilson told us later on a Spark roundtable call. "She looked like I had congratulated her on being grounded with zero screen time for the duration of her adolescence."

He left it there with Olivia, and watched her go to her desk and sit down like she hadn't just spent months working toward a near-unreachable goal that she'd managed to crush on her first try.

After class, he pulled her aside.

"Hey, can I ask you something?" Jack said. Olivia shrugged again. "Do you *like* basketball?"

Olivia gave him a look like he'd asked the dumbest question she'd ever heard ("I have my own teenagers at home. I'm used to it," Jack told us).

"Of course I like it," she said.

"I'm just checking, because you didn't seem that excited when I congratulated you earlier."

Olivia stuck to her story. "I like it. It's what my sister does."

Jack tried a different angle. "I know you're good at it. And being good at something feels good. Especially if you're living up to, or exceeding, expectations. But that feeling isn't the same as really *liking* it."

Something flashed in Olivia's eyes—but then she was back to her nonchalant self. "I know, but I do like it," she said.

Jack wished her a great afternoon and watched her walk out of the classroom. "There she was, this kid with a talent everyone else who tried out would do anything for. And she was acting like it was no big deal," Jack told us on the roundtable call. "Like it was a foregone conclusion that she was going to be a star basketball player, just like her sister. I figured that was the last I'd hear about it."

To his surprise, the very next morning, Olivia walked up to his desk before class.

"How do I know if I like something?" she asked.

His suspicion had been right on the money. And it was no wonder: with the years of teaching experience Jack had under his belt, he could spot a student who wasn't lit up by what they were doing a mile away.

The opposite was also true. "When a student finds their spark and dives into it, it's like they become the best version of themselves," he said to us. "In my experience, helping a student find their spark is one of the best things I can do to build trust and connection with them."

WHAT MAKES YOU BRILLIANT?

I've referred to the spark you have the opportunity to ignite in every student in your classroom, the spark that comes from deep within you and ripples throughout everyone you touch.

What does that spark look like?

You probably know what it *feels* like: that wonderful glow of doing work you love, being in flow, ending the day energized and feeling great about what you accomplished. The spark is in those moments when you don't even notice the time passing, and what you're doing no longer feels like work. The deep enjoyment and satisfaction of your work causes time to fly past—you look up at the clock on the wall and think, *yikes—it's time to head home already!*

As a teacher, finding your spark and focusing as much time and energy into that place where you're uniquely passionate and productive is of paramount importance. The spark of each of your students begins with you—and by finding yours, you can help them find theirs too.

Many students make it all the way through their school years without discovering what truly lights them up. Their "spark"—the unique intersection where talent meets passion—often remains hidden. One of the biggest challenges is scale; teachers work with dozens, sometimes hundreds, of students at a time, making it difficult to provide the individual attention needed to help each student uncover their strengths. And even when teachers want to create these opportunities, they often lack the tools or training to do so. Helping students identify their passions isn't just about asking the right questions—it's about creating an environment that encourages curiosity and exploration.

Right now, the knowledge and systems for helping students find their spark aren't common in schools. But they could be. With the right leadership and a commitment to fostering student growth, we can create educational environments where every student has the chance to discover their unique strengths—and the confidence to pursue them. That's the power of Spark in the classroom.

From the moment children enter school, they begin to evaluate themselves in comparison to their peers. It happens subtly at first, but it doesn't take long for patterns to emerge. Kids quickly categorize themselves based on academic performance, particularly in reading and math. These early markers—standardized test scores, spelling quizzes, and math evaluations—become the foundation for how students perceive their own potential. By first or second grade, many children have internalized an identity tied to their perceived academic standing. They know which reading group they're in, and they're acutely aware of what it means.

"Blue group, red group, yellow group," educators might say, as though the names or colors conceal the hierarchy. But kids aren't fooled. They know that the blue group is for the "smart kids," and that these labels come with assumptions—assumptions they carry with them from year to year.

These identities stick. They're reinforced by comments, test scores, and the information passed between teachers: "This student is advanced," or "This one needs extra support." For many children, this labeling process defines their potential in their own eyes. And without intervention, these beliefs about themselves often remain fixed, shaping how they engage with school and the world.

But what if there was another way? What if, instead of being solely defined by test scores or reading groups, children were encouraged to discover their unique sparks—the interests, talents, or passions that make them feel alive and capable?

The power of recognizing and nurturing sparks can't be overstated. A spark is something that excites a child, something they're naturally drawn to, whether it's art, storytelling, problem-solving, or building things with their hands. Sparks allow students to see themselves outside of rigid academic categories. They provide an avenue for kids to say, "I'm good at something," with all the confidence and self-esteem that comes with it; and that realization can transform how they view their place in the world.

As Monica puts it: "There's a genius in every child. It's our job to help them find it."

Finding sparks requires intentionality from educators. It means looking beyond test scores and standardized benchmarks to ask deeper questions: *What excites this student? What makes them lose track of time? How can I integrate their interests into the classroom?*

For many students, the simple act of having a teacher notice and nurture their spark can be life-changing. When educators focus on building connections and fostering curiosity, they ignite a sense of possibility within their students. They help them see that their worth isn't confined to a single measure but is as diverse and limitless as their potential.

Ultimately, this is what Spark is about: shifting the focus from where students fall on a predetermined scale to who they are as *individuals*. It's about asking, "What makes you come alive?" and then doing everything possible to help that spark grow.

STUDENTS SPEAK

"With Spark, we learn how to advocate for ourselves in different ways. We also learn to build more confidence because other people start to understand the way we see things."

WHEN THE SPARKS AREN'T OBVIOUS

Right off the bat, I'll bet you're wondering: why do you need to help students *find* their spark? Isn't it obvious what it is?

Well, no. Not always. In fact, it often takes some detective work.

First of all, research has shown that two-thirds of people have no meaningful awareness of what their true strengths are.[20] (If that's you, you're in good company, and that's probably a sign to start looking.)

Have you ever taken a strengths assessment? I have. Dozens of them, actually. They're useful in that you're able to quickly get a glance at where you should be focusing your efforts to maximize productivity and results.

However, they're not much help in maximizing *happiness*.

It's one thing to know your strengths, but your greatest potential—the furthest reaches of your positive number line—lies in the strengths that *energize* you. Your greatest potential lies not just in your talents, but in your unique brilliance.

Cultivating and activating your unique strengths is a key practice of Positive Psychology. The VIA Institute on Character, founded by Positive Psychology researcher Dr. Neal Mayerson, funded a team of fifty-five social scientists to study world cultures, philosophies, and psychology to identify core human virtues—the traits associated with the positive end of the number line. Led by Dr. Martin Seligman and Dr. Christopher Peterson, this team crafted a list of twenty-four positive human traits that spans all cultures, nationalities, and time periods. They consider each individual's top character strengths to be defined by three key elements:[21]

---

20 Dr. Ryan Niemiec, "What Are Your Signature Strengths?" VIA Institute on Character, March 23, 2012, https://www.viacharacter.org/topics/articles/what-are-your-signature-strengths.

21 Peterson and Seligman, Character Strengths and Virtues.

1. **Essential:** This strength feels essential to who you are as a person.

2. **Effortless:** When you use this strength, it feels natural and effortless.

3. **Energizing:** Using this strength energizes and uplifts you. It leaves you feeling happy, in balance, and ready to take on more.

This holds even more true for kids—as any teacher or parent who has tried to get a kid to focus on *anything* besides their current hobby or preferred activity has experienced.

There's a unique magic that happens when students get the chance to work on things they're good at. Their eyes light up, their energy shifts, and their engagement levels soar. They're not just having fun or excelling academically—they're tapping into their natural spark. Research shows that when teachers help students discover and use their strengths, the impact goes far beyond grades; it creates excitement, engagement, and a sense of fulfillment that can transform their entire educational journey.

A study published in *The Journal of Positive Psychology* reveals that focusing on strengths in education leads to enhanced student engagement and better academic outcomes. Instead of focusing solely on fixing weaknesses, teachers who tap into and celebrate student strengths create an environment of positivity and possibility. Students are more likely to see school as a place where they can shine, not just struggle. When that happens, their motivation skyrockets, and their sense of belonging grows.

This is more important than ever with today's students, who report some of the lowest engagement levels ever seen. According to a survey from the Walton Family Foundation and Gallup, between 25% and 54% of students say they are not having engaging experiences in school—like feeling that what they are learning is important or interesting.[22] Less than half of students say their schoolwork positively challenges them or aligns with what they do best.

When it comes to K-12 classrooms, how engaged they feel isn't just about how much they like school—it's a huge factor in their overall well-being and how they see their future. The 25% of students who rate their engagement the highest are doing way better than their less-engaged peers. These students are more than twice as likely to be thriving in their lives (76% compared to 32%). Even more striking, they're over four times as likely to strongly believe they have a great future ahead of them (61% vs. 15%). That's a *huge* deal.

Students who don't plan to pursue college after high school are far less likely to feel motivated by or interested in what they're learning. They're also less likely to say their schoolwork gives them a chance to shine and do what they're best at. This gap matters because when students don't feel connected to what they're learning, it's hard for them to see school as meaningful or as a stepping stone to something bigger.

These numbers tell a powerful story: engagement in the classroom isn't just a "nice-to-have." It's directly tied to how students feel about themselves and their future. And when we create environments where students feel motivated, interested, and like their strengths matter, we're not just teaching them lessons—we're helping them believe in their potential.

As one of our Spark teachers said on a recent roundtable call: "Our students need wins in life. They need to be reminded of their strengths

---

22 https://news.gallup.com/poll/648896/schools-struggle-engage-gen-students.aspx

and how those strengths bring light to the entire class."

MY BIG SPARK

From the time I was a little girl, I've always been fascinated by people—how they act, react, and interact. Throughout my school years, I took advantage of any opportunity I could find to study psychology, and eventually, at Duke, majored in the field. I loved *everything* about psychology. I was never bored.

But then, my senior year of college, companies came to campus to recruit for the next year—and I got waylaid one day by an investment banking firm who painted me a glamorous picture of New York finance life. At that age, when we're all at the beginning of building our lives and we're hungry to feel accomplished and respectable, banking seemed like something I "should" do, the kind of career I'd be an idiot to turn down. So I interviewed, got a job at an investment firm, and moved to NYC.

This is where, in an 80s movie montage, you'd see twenty-two-year-old Jackie excitedly imagining herself sitting down in conference rooms and dramatically counting her stacks of cash…and then screen wipe to scenes of stark reality, where she's chained to a dreary cubicle, eating crappy takeout for every meal, crashing into bed in her tiny hole of an apartment at an ungodly time each night, barely kicking off her shoes in her exhaustion. Yeah. It was all of three months before I realized I'd made a mistake. I'm generally *very* quick to notice when I'm miserable, and boy, did that job make me miserable.

One day while rushing to a corner deli down the street during the fifteen minutes I had for lunch, I caught a glimpse of myself in a shop window and stopped dead. I looked tired, defeated, totally *done*.

Right there on the street, I burst into tears. I stood sobbing despondently into my hands, the busy city around me taking absolutely *no* notice. (That's not a movie cliché—New Yorkers are pretty accustomed to people having breakdowns in public. Just another Tuesday in the Big Apple.)

What am I doing? I asked myself. This isn't what I wanted.

Was I good at the job? Yes. Absolutely. I was good with numbers, I could do math, and I was a hard worker.

Was I happy? Was I fulfilled? *Heck no.* Day in and day out, I sat behind a desk by myself for fourteen hours crunching numbers in spreadsheets. It was somehow mind-numbing and stressful at the same time. I didn't have any work friends; I didn't even have time to try to make any, with my blink-and-you'll-miss-it lunch break. It was just me and Excel in a numbers battle from sunup to sundown. I was in my apartment for so little time each day that I couldn't keep a plant alive, let alone relax or try to have a social life. The only other person I ever saw outside of work was my roommate, in passing, as we squeezed by each other in and out of our tiny windowless bathroom.

Standing there sobbing in the busiest city in the world, people bumping and elbowing me as they passed, I'd never felt so alone.

Until another New Yorker actually reached out with compassion.

It was Fred, the man who camped in front of the corner deli and could often be found hanging out on the front steps of our office building. Fred came up next to me and put his arm around my shoulders. Any other day, I'd probably have been freaked out at a stranger initiating physical contact in the middle of the sidewalk. But as lonely and hopeless as I felt, I didn't shrink away from Fred.

He patted my shoulder and said simply, "It's gonna be okay."

It's amazing how the smallest moments can sometimes make the biggest impact. That was a life-changing moment for me. It was the moment I realized that my life, my career, my current predicament with what I'd found to be a soul-sucking job, and even the emotional state I was in were all *choices*.

This is a choice, I thought. *I have a choice. I get to decide what happens next.*

"Thank you," I said shakily to Fred. I gave him the money I was going to use for my lunch and turned around, went straight upstairs to the office, and quit on the spot.

It was hasty, and probably an irrational move, because I didn't have another job lined up or even any prospects. But I was suddenly so clear on what I had to do. I had to make a choice to go after happiness. I had to choose fulfillment. I had to find my spark, the livelihood that I was not just good at, but that also energized me.

I was good at my job. But I didn't *like* it.

My boss at the firm (who hated me anyway) nodded as though she wasn't surprised, gave me a cursory "We'll mail you your last check; good luck," and that was it. I was out.

I went back downstairs into the sunny afternoon, wiping tear tracks from my face and smiling for the first time in weeks. Fred had moved on to another block, perhaps to drop some wisdom on another sobbing young person who was questioning their life choices. I walked home to the apartment I could no longer afford feeling lighter than air.

From there, I'd like to say I immediately found my passion, the career that lit my spark, but it wasn't as straightforward as that—the line was pretty squiggly throughout the rest of my twenties as it led me to graduate school at Harvard, then to Tickle.com writing online quizzes, and then deeper and deeper into the realm of Positive Psychology and human behavior. Through it all, though, I was led by a new determination. I was going to find my spark. I was going to prioritize happiness, fulfillment, being lit from within by the work I was doing. As long as I followed that drive, I couldn't go wrong.

THE SHIFT INTO BRILLIANCE

Helping Olivia find her spark didn't happen overnight, as Jack told us. "She was totally wrapped up in this pre-ordained identity that had been passed down from her sister. She was a great basketball player, period, and there was nothing else to her."

Jack started by describing the feeling of flow when he himself worked on hobbies that lit him up. "I said all the stuff about time dropping away, getting lost in it, wanting to get back to it more than anything else. She seemed unconvinced. So then I just asked her to do something: pay attention to where she spent her time."

He tasked Olivia with writing down each night everything she'd done that day that was her choice to do, not a previous obligation—not school, basketball practice, homework, or family time. Olivia did it the entire week, and on Friday she approached him with a nervous look on her face.

"Did you write down all the stuff you did that you didn't have to do?" he asked her.

She nodded, but looked like she knew she was about to fail a test. "It's only one thing." She handed over the list.

Hung out with friends. She had dutifully written it down for each day she'd recorded, but it was indeed just one thing.

"That's it?" Jack said. "You didn't read, or watch a show, or watch YouTube, or anything?"

"Not really," she replied. "I'm boring."

"I doubt that," Jack said, internally cracking up at the idea that this multi-talented teenager who was crushing school and sports thought she was *boring*. "Let me ask you this: when you and your friends hang out, what kind of stuff do you do?"

Here, he saw that same *something* flash across Olivia's eyes. Excitement?

"Oh, we do tons of stuff," she said. "Like yesterday, we went to this skate park and watched some guys do tricks. And on Tuesday we went downtown and checked out this new mural..." As she talked, she was digging in her pocket for her phone. She pulled it out, opened it up, and handed it over to him.

It was open to her Instagram account, and Jack was immediately stunned. The photos he was looking at were incredible. Olivia had documented what seemed like every second of the past several days hanging out with her friends, but the photos weren't just your typical snaps. They were artfully composed, dynamic, *beautiful*.

"You took all these pictures?" he said—and once again earned himself the *duh!* look from Olivia.

"Yeah," she said. "I always take pics when I'm hanging out with people. Sometimes I just walk around my neighborhood and take random pics of stuff. Cars. Flowers. I don't know, whatever looks good."

"Would you say you like photography more than you like playing basketball?" he asked her.

"And then I watched her finally put the pieces together," Jack told us on the roundtable. "It had literally never occurred to Olivia that taking pictures for her Instagram was *photography*. She saw it as just the same social media stuff her friends were doing. She had never taken it seriously."

He smiled, remembering. "The next parent-teacher conference was heartwarming and validating. Her mom came up to me and said, "Oh, so you're the one who got my daughter to beg us for a fancy camera!" She was joking, though. It was completely obvious to everyone what actually lit Olivia up. Once she joined the Photography Club and got a real camera, you never saw her without the thing."

SPARK STUDY RESULTS

Our independent Spark study showed tremendous improvements in teacher burnout rates. Here are a few key results:

- Teachers at the Spark school were half as likely to report feelings of **work breaking them down** (63.9% at the control school, versus only 29.4% at the Spark school).

- Teachers at the Spark school were half as likely to feel **frustrated by their work** (59.7% at the control school, versus only 29.4% at the Spark school).

- A *really* stunning result: teachers at the Spark school responded that they were **"feeling at the end of my rope"** at a rate 40.3% less than at the control school (56.9% at the control school, versus only 14.7% at the Spark school).

RANDOM PATTERNS OF LIGHT

When I think of what makes a sparkler beautiful, I think of the randomness and unpredictability of the sparks.

Your eyes don't know where the next bright shimmer is going to come from—it's just a cloud of glowy sparkle shooting off in all directions. Each spark is unique in its size, shape, and trajectory. Together, they create the full effect.

This is also how I think of brilliance in the classroom. The most engaged classrooms are the ones that include many different sparks harmonizing into a fiery light show.

As a teacher, your role is to guide and nurture the natural spark not only within yourself, but within each of your students. This will also organically strengthen the performance of your entire classroom—to get the absolute best out of each of them individually and as a group.

Helping students discover their strengths doesn't have to be a huge, complicated process. It's really just adding a few simple practices into your day-to-day teaching. Spark focuses on making small but powerful changes that let students feel seen and excited about their learning. Here's how you can do it:

Project Reflection (Individually)

Wrap up projects or activities by getting students to reflect on their experiences. Try questions like:

- What part of this project did you enjoy the most?

- What part was most challenging?

- If you could do it again, what would you do differently?

Let students share their thoughts without worrying about "right" answers. This reflection isn't about grading—it's about helping them understand themselves better.

Give Students Roles in Group Work

Before starting a group project, list out the roles (like researcher, presenter, or organizer) and explain what each one involves. Ask students, "Which role do you think fits you best?" Giving them ownership helps them feel more invested and lets them lean into their strengths.

If someone's unsure, suggest trying a role they've never done before. It's a low-stakes way for them to explore new skills.

Group Reflection (as a Class)

After a project, spend time as a class talking about what worked well within project groups, and what could be better next time. Include questions like:

- How did your group work together?

- What role did you take on, and did you learn something new about yourself?

- If you did the project again, would you want to keep the role you had, or try a new role?

This is a great bonding activity for students, but it also has a profound psychological effect and impact on their future outcomes. This is because of a concept called *metacognition*—thinking about your own thinking—and the influence it has on learning. Research shows that teaching students how to reflect on their learning significantly improves academic performance, and that metacognition strategies, like goal-setting, self-monitoring, and self-reflection, have a positive effect on future performance.[23]

Call out when you see students using their unique talents—whether it's problem-solving, creativity, or keeping the group on track. Let them know their contributions matter. These small steps create a big impact. When students realize their contributions matter, they're more likely to show up with curiosity and confidence. And when teachers take the time to guide that discovery, the whole classroom becomes a place where sparks can thrive.

Great teachers develop strengths. *Exceptional* teachers develop sparks.

23   Hester de Boer, Anouk S. Donker,Danny D.N.M. Kostons,Greetje P.C. van der Werf. *Long-term effects of metacognitive strategy instruction on student academic performance: A meta-analysis.* Educational Research Review, June 2018.

CLASSROOM ACTION PLAN: UNCOVER THEIR SPARKS

Ask your students If you could spend all day doing one thing, what would you do? They could draw this or write it!

Ask your students: Think about all the subjects and activities you do at school. What is your favorite thing to learn? What do you enjoy about it?

Ask your students: When you're not in school, what are some things you love learning about? How do you learn about them (books, videos, hands-on experiences, etc.)?

Scan here for a downloadable action plan you can take into the classroom!